Peterson
First Guide
to
INSECTS
of North America

Christopher Leahy

Illustrated by
Richard E. White

Based on
A Field Guide to the Insects of North America,
by Donald J. Borror and Richard E. White

HOUGE   Y

Boston   New York

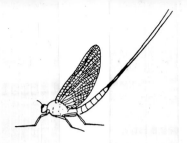

Selected illustrations reproduced from *A Field Guide to
the Insects of America North of Mexico,* copyright © 1970
by Donald J. Borror and Richard E. White, and from *A
Field Guide to the Beetles of North America,* copyright ©
1983 by Richard E. White.
   The illustrations on pp. 55, 87, 89, 91, 93, 107, 108,
and 119 were prepared for this First Guide by Amy
Wright.

Library of Congress Cataloging-in-Publication Data
Leahy, Christopher W.
   Peterson first guide to insects of North America.
   Cover title: Peterson first guides. Insects. "Based on a
field guide to the insects of America north of Mexico by
Donald J. Borror and Richard E. White." Includes index.
   1. Insects—United States—Identification.
   2. Insects—Canada—Identification.
   I. Borror, Donald Joyce, 1907–
Field guide to the insects of America north of Mexico.
II. Title. III. Title: First guide to insects of North America.
IV. Title: Peterson first guides. Insects.
QL474.L43 1987 595.70973 86-21374
ISBN 978-0-395-90664-4

Printed in China

SCP 32 31
4500722336

Editor's Note

In 1934, my *Field Guide to the Birds* first saw the light of day. This book was designed so that live birds could be readily identified at a distance, by their patterns, shapes, and field marks, without resorting to the technical points specialists use to name species in the hand or in the specimen tray. The book introduced the "Peterson System," as it is now called, a visual system based on patternistic drawings with arrows to pinpoint the key field marks. The system is now used throughout the Peterson Field Guide Series, which has grown to over thirty volumes on a wide range of subjects, from ferns to fishes, rocks to stars, animal tracks to edible plants.

Even though Peterson Field Guides are intended for the novice as well as the expert, there are still many beginners who would like something simpler to start with—a smaller guide that would give them confidence. It is for this audience—those who perhaps recognize a crow or robin, buttercup or daisy, but little else—that the Peterson First Guides have been created. They offer a selection of the animals and plants you are most likely to see during your first forays afield. By narrowing the choices—and using the Peterson System— they make identification much easier. First Guides make it easy to get started in the field, and easy to graduate to the full-fledged Peterson Field Guides.

Roger Tory Peterson

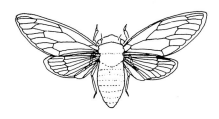

Introducing the Insects

The first trick to mastering insect identification is to concentrate on distinguishing the large groupings called *orders.* You will probably find that many orders are already familiar to you. One order, for example, contains all the beetles, another all the flies, and so forth. In many cases, you will also recognize the *families* of insects into which the orders are divided. The many species of lightningbugs, for instance, make up a family within the beetle order.

By the time you are concentrating on the *species* in a particular family, you will have long since graduated to a more detailed book, such as *A Field Guide to Beetles of North America* in the Peterson Field Guide Series. But this *First Guide to Insects* is designed to get you started, and therefore focuses on the larger groups—the orders and families. Even so, you may sometimes find that you can identify a species from the illustration representing a family.

Refer to the identification chart on pp. 9–13 to determine the order or group to which the insect you have seen may belong. The larger orders are broken down into families. Once you have decided on an order or family for your insect, turn to the page where that group is discussed. You will find a description of features you may use to identify the members of that order or family, along with information on habitat, behavior, and other details. On the facing page, arrows on the illustrations point to the distinguishing features emphasized in the text.

If, after a careful comparison with all the illustrations, you still cannot place your insect in an order, it probably belongs to one of the many less common groups of insects that have been omitted from this introductory book. To identify it, you will have to look in a more comprehensive book, such as *A Field Guide to the Insects of America North of Mexico, A Field Guide to the Butterflies,* or *A Field Guide to Moths of Eastern North America* in the Peterson Field Guide series.

Observing Insects

One of the many advantages of having an interest in insects is that you can pursue it virtually any time and any place. Two habitats where you will find insects particularly abundant are old fields containing a variety of plants, and old, clean ponds or slow-flowing rivers. Good insect hunting can be found in many other habitats as well. An ordinary garden, the lights of a downtown parking lot at night, your wood pile, and an unkempt corner of an abandoned lot all have communities of insects.

It is possible to find insects all year long, even in the North. However, insect life is at its most active in warm weather. In parts of the country with a prolonged winter, you will find the greatest variety of species from midsummer to early autumn.

Observing insect habits can be even more rewarding than the traditional pursuit of killing and mounting specimens. You can easily fill a notebook simply by recording all the different insect activities that take place on a single goldenrod plant in an afternoon. Keeping a live caterpillar or other immature insect in captivity, along with a supply of its proper food, allows you to watch the often astonishing process of insect metamorphosis. Be sure the container you use as a cage is not too small, has an adequate supply of air, and is not allowed to get very hot or very cold. Keep a record of the place where you found the insect, and the plant it was on or near. Release the insect in the same place where you found it when you have finished observing it.

Note: The actual size of most insects illustrated is shown by a line near the drawing; for some large insects this line is in two sections. These lines generally represent body length (from front of the head to tip of the abdomen, or to the wingtips if they extend beyond the abdomen).

Life Stages

Insects' lives are divided into a series of stages: egg, one or more immature stages, and adult. In most cases, the appearance of a given species changes drastically in each successive stage. The process by which one stage transforms into another is called metamorphosis. There are two basic types of metamorphosis; each has many variations.

In simple metamorphosis, a nymph hatches from the egg. It grows to adulthood through a series of increases in size. In some groups, such as the true bugs (p. 36), the nymphs change very little in appearance as they grow. They differ from the adults mainly in size, coloration, and the lack of wings if the adults are winged. Immature bugs (nymphs) also live in the same habitat as the adults and eat the same food.

Many aquatic insects, such as dragonflies, stoneflies, and mayflies, also undergo simple metamorphosis, but their nymphs and adults differ in appearance, habitat, and food types.

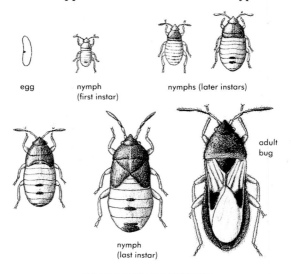

egg

nymph
(first instar)

nymphs (later instars)

adult
bug

nymph
(last instar)

SIMPLE METAMORPHOSIS
(OF A BUG)

In complete metamorphosis, a wormlike form called a larva hatches from the egg. As it grows, its form remains the same, though its size increases greatly and its coloration may change. When the larva is fully grown, it transforms into a pupa, which looks like a simple, segmented capsule or a little mummy with many features of the adult visible on the surface. Many moths and other insects spin a fibrous cocoon around the pupa. The pupa does not feed, and remains in a dormant state for a period of weeks or months. Many species overwinter as pupae. The adult that emerges from the pupa does not resemble either the larva or the pupa.

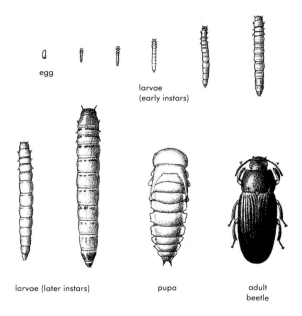

egg

larvae
(early instars)

larvae (later instars)   pupa   adult
                                                                   beetle

COMPLETE METAMORPHOSIS
(OF A BEETLE)

Parts of Insects

The identification of insects is based to a great
extent on external features. There are names
for even the smallest details and subdivisions
of an insect's body. Most of these names are
technical, and the details may be hard to
observe. Since the aim of this book is to help
the reader to recognize only the more common
orders and families of insects, reference to
most of these anatomical fine points has been
omitted.

Nevertheless, a general knowledge of an
insect's body is useful in distinguishing the
major groups, and there are many peculiar-
looking insect appendages about which you
will naturally be curious.

The outside of an insect's body is its skeleton. It is made not of bone like the human
skeleton, but of a light, relatively hard, but
generally flexible material called chitin. This
skeleton is divided into three parts: the head,
thorax, and abdomen. Most insects have a pair
of antennae on the head. Antennae vary in
length, shape, and number of jointed segments. Wings and legs grow from the thorax.
Females of many species also have an ovipositor at the tip of the abdomen, with which they
deposit eggs.

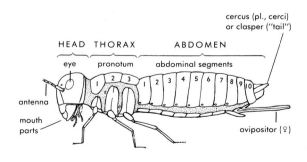

The following chart shows the major orders of insects. For convenience, they are divided into two big groups: those with wings and those without wings.

1	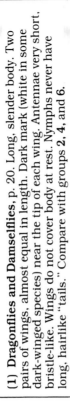	Most of these insects have large, usually transparent wings that are conspicuous when folded. (1) **Dragonflies and Damselflies,** p. 20. Long, slender body. Two pairs of wings, almost equal in length. Dark mark (white in some dark-winged species) near the tip of each wing. Antennae very short, bristle-like. Wings do not cover body at rest. Nymphs never have long, hairlike "tails." Compare with groups **2, 4,** and **6.**
2		(2) **Mayflies,** p. 17. Two pairs of wings (rarely one pair). Hind wings much shorter than forewings. Wings held vertically over the back at rest. Adults and nymphs have 3 (rarely 2) long, hairlike "tails" extending from the tip of the abdomen. Antennae very short and bristle-like. Compare with female ichneumon wasps (p. 111), and with groups **1** and **3.**

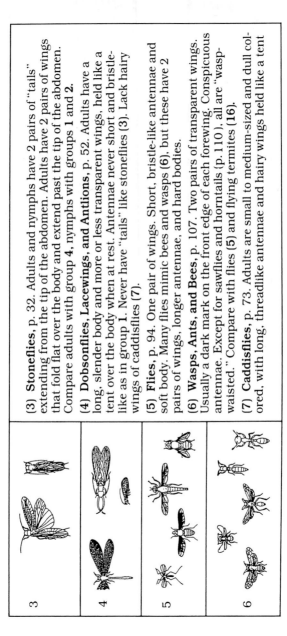

3	(3) **Stoneflies**, p. 32. Adults and nymphs have 2 pairs of "tails" extending from the tip of the abdomen. Adults have 2 pairs of wings that fold flat over the body and extend past the tip of the abdomen. Compare adults with groups **1** and **2**. nymphs with groups **1** and **2**.
4	(4) **Dobsonflies, Lacewings, and Antlions**, p. 52. Adults have a long, slender body and more or less transparent wings, held like a tent over the body when at rest. Antennae never short and bristle-like as in group **1**. Never have "tails" like stoneflies (**3**). Lack hairy wings of caddisflies (**7**).
5	(5) **Flies**, p. 94. One pair of wings. Short, bristle-like antennae and soft body. Many flies mimic bees and wasps (**6**), but these have 2 pairs of wings, longer antennae, and hard bodies.
6	(6) **Wasps, Ants, and Bees**, p. 107. Two pairs of transparent wings. Usually a dark mark on the front edge of each forewing. Conspicuous antennae. Except for sawflies and horntails (p. 110), all are "wasp-waisted." Compare with flies (**5**) and flying termites (**16**).
	(7) **Caddisflies**, p. 73. Adults are small to medium-sized and dull colored, with long, threadlike antennae and hairy wings held like a tent

7	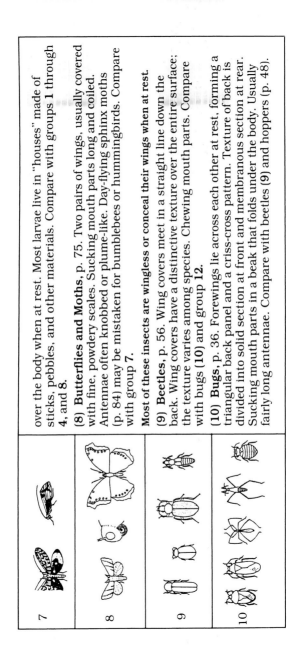	over the body when at rest. Most larvae live in "houses" made of sticks, pebbles, and other materials. Compare with groups **1** through **4**, and **8**.
8		**(8) Butterflies and Moths,** p. 75. Two pairs of wings, usually covered with fine, powdery scales. Sucking mouth parts long and coiled. Day-flying sphinx moths (p. 84) may be mistaken for bumblebees or hummingbirds. Compare with group **7**.
		Most of these insects are wingless or conceal their wings when at rest.
9		**(9) Beetles,** p. 56. Wing covers meet in a straight line down the back. Wing covers have a distinctive texture over the entire surface; the texture varies among species. Chewing mouth parts. Compare with bugs (**10**) and group **12**.
10		**(10) Bugs,** p. 36. Forewings lie across each other at rest, forming a triangular back panel and a criss-cross pattern. Texture of back is divided into solid section at front and membranous section at rear. Sucking mouth parts in a beak that folds under the body. Usually fairly long antennae. Compare with beetles (**9**) and hoppers (p. 48).

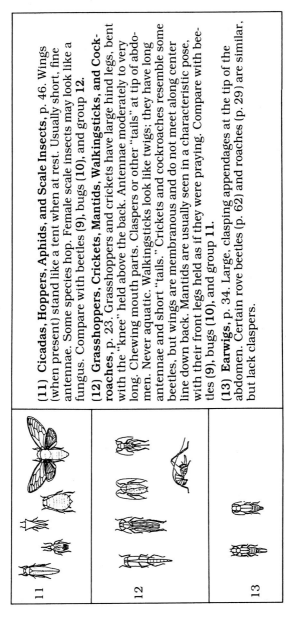

[11] Cicadas, Hoppers, Aphids, and Scale Insects, p. 46. Wings (when present) stand like a tent when at rest. Usually short, fine antennae. Some species hop. Female scale insects may look like a fungus. Compare with beetles (9), bugs (10), and group **12**.

[12] Grasshoppers, Crickets, Mantids, Walkingsticks, and Cockroaches, p. 23. Grasshoppers and crickets have large hind legs, bent with the "knee" held above the back. Antennae moderately to very long. Chewing mouth parts. Claspers or other "tails" at tip of abdomen. Never aquatic. Walkingsticks look like twigs; they have long antennae and short "tails." Crickets and cockroaches resemble some beetles, but wings are membranous and do not meet along center line down back. Mantids are usually seen in a characteristic pose, with their front legs held as if they were praying. Compare with beetles (9), bugs (10), and group **11**.

[13] Earwigs, p. 34. Large, clasping appendages at the tip of the abdomen. Certain rove beetles (p. 62) and roaches (p. 29) are similar, but lack claspers.

14	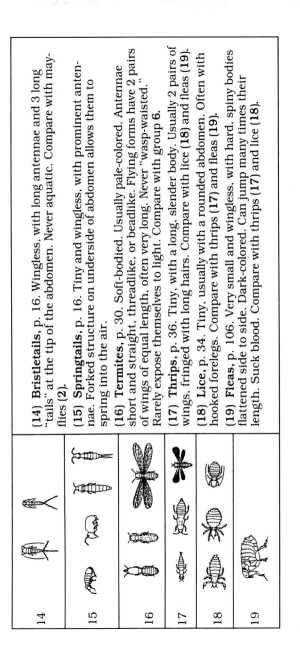	**(14) Bristletails,** p. 16. Wingless, with long antennae and 3 long "tails" at the tip of the abdomen. Never aquatic. Compare with mayflies **(2)**.
15		**(15) Springtails,** p. 16. Tiny and wingless, with prominent antennae. Forked structure on underside of abdomen allows them to spring into the air.
16		**(16) Termites,** p. 30. Soft-bodied. Usually pale-colored. Antennae short and straight, threadlike, or beadlike. Flying forms have 2 pairs of wings of equal length, often very long. Never "wasp-waisted." Rarely expose themselves to light. Compare with group **6**.
17		**(17) Thrips,** p. 36. Tiny, with a long, slender body. Usually 2 pairs of wings, fringed with long hairs. Compare with lice **(18)** and fleas **(19)**.
18		**(18) Lice,** p. 34. Tiny, usually with a rounded abdomen. Often with hooked forelegs. Compare with thrips **(17)** and fleas **(19)**.
19		**(19) Fleas,** p. 106. Very small and wingless, with hard, spiny bodies flattened side to side. Dark-colored. Can jump many times their length. Suck blood. Compare with thrips **(17)** and lice **(18)**.

Some Common Insect-like Creatures

SOWBUGS rather resemble tiny armadillos. They are often abundant under logs and in other dark, damp places. Like crabs and lobsters, they are crustaceans. They might be mistaken for a kind of beetle, but note their *7 pairs* of leg-like appendages. Beetles, like all insects, have *only 3* pairs of legs. Some sowbugs roll up into a ball when disturbed and are therefore called pillbugs.

MILLIPEDES are common in soil and debris and under stones, logs, and bark. You might mistake them for caterpillars or other types of insect larvae. However, millipedes have 2 pairs of legs on most of their many body segments, for a total of *30 or more pairs.* Insect larvae never have as many as this.

CENTIPEDES are common inhabitants of rotten wood, leaf litter, and similar sheltered places. Like millipedes, centipedes resemble some insect larvae. However, centipedes have at least *15 pairs* of legs, one pair per segment, more than any insect. Most North American centipedes are quite small, but in the South and West some species reach 6 inches in length. Because of the poisons they use to immobilize their prey, these large centipedes can deliver a very painful bite.

ARACHNIDS include scorpions, spiders, daddy-long-legs, ticks, and mites. All of these have *4 pairs* of legs, and several have *2 claw-like appendages,* called palps, that look like a fifth pair. Water striders and other leggy insects look a little like spiders, and some bugs and beetles resemble ticks. But adult insects that have legs always have 3, and *only 3,* pairs of legs.

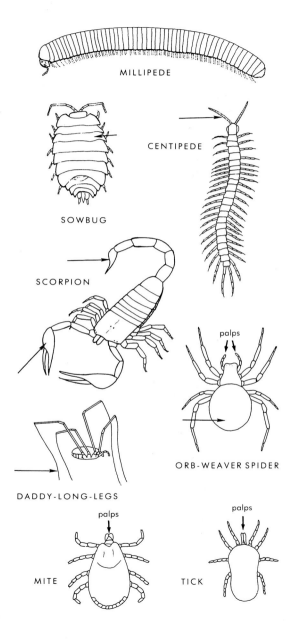

MILLIPEDE

SOWBUG

CENTIPEDE

SCORPION

palps

ORB-WEAVER SPIDER

DADDY-LONG-LEGS

palps

MITE

palps

TICK

Insects

SPRINGTAILS are tiny, *wingless* insects with fairly *prominent antennae* and usually a *forked structure* on the underside of the abdomen, which allows them to spring into the air. They vary widely in form. Springtails are among the most abundant creatures on earth, and occur by the millions per acre. Though most people are not aware of them, springtails are immensely beneficial in breaking down leaf litter and fungi into soil components. A few species are minor garden pests. The most familiar springtails are the "snowfleas" that cover the snow during winter thaws.

BRISTLETAILS are *wingless*, crawling, terrestrial insects with *long, segmented antennae* and *3 longs "tails"* extending from the tip of the abdomen. (Mayfly larvae have 3 "tails," but are strictly aquatic.) You may have seen silverfish or firebrats in your basement or in similar dark, damp places. Other bristletails live outdoors in leaf litter or under stones. House-inhabiting species eat starchy substances and may damage stored books, wallpaper, clothing, and starchy vegetables. In nature, they eat decaying plants. These are among the most primitive of living insects.

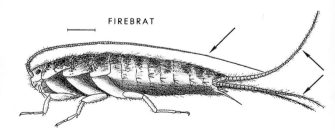

FIREBRAT

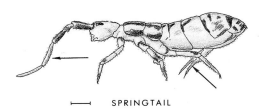

SPRINGTAIL

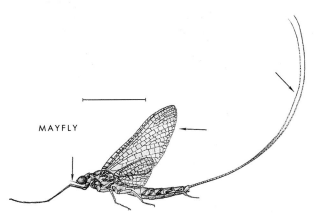

MAYFLY

MAYFLIES. Adult mayflies can be distinguished from all other insects by the presence of *2 (rarely 1) pairs* of transparent wings of *unequal length,* held *vertically together over the back* when the insect is at rest, and *3 (rarely 2) long, hairlike "tails"* extending from the tip of the abdomen. The antennae are *very short* and *bristle-like.* There may be a single pair of wings, and 2 tails.

Adult mayflies are small to medium-sized insects, with very soft bodies. They are not colorful, but their wings and bodies are often attractively patterned in rich browns, yellows, or white. They are uncommonly delicate and graceful.

Mayfly nymphs are among the most abundant forms of aquatic life. They live in all types of clean, fresh water. Some burrow several inches into mud, some crawl over bottom litter or swim actively, and some cling to rocks in fast currents. Because of their varied habits, there is much variation in their general appearance. All eat tiny aquatic plants and are eaten by a great many animals, including trout. They cannot live in water with low oxygen content, and are therefore good indicators of organic pollution.

When they mature, the nymphs of most species swim to the surface, and the winged form must escape from its nymphal skin and take flight immediately. This first winged form is called a subadult. It has cloudy wings and its eyes, legs, and genitalia are generally not fully developed. No other living insect develops wings before it has reached full maturity, an indication that mayflies are among the most primitive present-day insects.

Mayflies sometimes emerge from lakes and streams in enormous numbers. These events often trigger feeding frenzies in fish, and therefore provide exciting opportunities for fishermen. In fact, mayflies are the most popular models for artificial flies. The subadult mayflies fly up into trees or other places of shelter where they remain for a day or two. Then they molt again into the adult form, which has fully developed eyes, legs, and genitalia. Mayflies eat only as nymphs. Adults of most species live for a day or so. Some live for a month, and others for only a matter of hours. In many cases, males form aerial mating swarms to which the females come to be fertilized. Eggs are dropped onto the water, or the female may wade in and deposit them on the bottom.

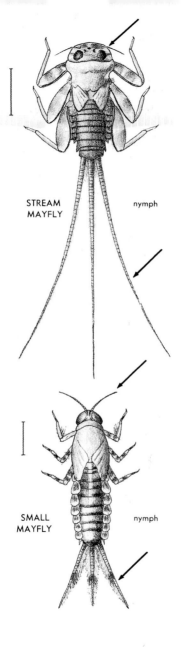

STREAM
MAYFLY

nymph

SMALL
MAYFLY

nymph

DRAGONFLIES AND DAMSELFLIES

have *long, slender bodies* with *2 pairs of wings,* of approximately equal length. No other insects with these general character- istics have the combination of a *prominent dark mark* (sometimes white in dark- winged species) near the tip of each wing, and very *short, bristle-like antennae.* The wings never conceal the abdomen when the insect is at rest. Dragonflies hold their wings out flat when they rest. Most damsel- flies hold their wings together above their backs when they rest. Compare them with antlions (p. 54), horntails (p. 110), and mayflies (p. 17).

Most members of this group lay clumps of eggs on the surface of the water or in plant tissue. The nymphs are among the most active predators of the aquatic world. Adults feed largely on flying insects. Some species of dragonflies eat large numbers of mosqui- toes. Large species can inflict a harmless bite. However, they neither sting nor sew up lips and ears. There are about 400 North American species in this group.

COMMON SKIMMERS are the dragonflies you are most likely to see around ponds and marshes. Many are *brightly colored—red, yellow,* or *green,* as well as pastel blue and gray. The wings of many are marked with *black* and *white* or tinted *yellow* or *orange.* You may see pairs flying together in prepa- ration for mating or egg laying, with the male holding the female by the neck and leading her around.

DARNERS are mostly *large,* strong-flying drag- onflies, usually brightly and distinctively patterned in *blue* and *green.* They typically patrol margins of ponds, lakes, and marshes, and seldom alight except to roost for the night. The Green Darner migrates between breeding areas in the North and South.

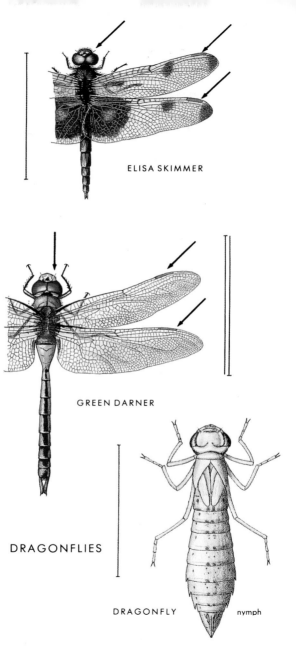

ELISA SKIMMER

GREEN DARNER

DRAGONFLIES

DRAGONFLY nymph

NARROW-WINGED DAMSELFLIES. Most damselflies belong to this family, and virtually no body of fresh water is without at least a few. Perhaps the most familiar are the "bluets." Other species are bright red, yellow, green, or some combination of colors. The vast majority are *clear-winged.* They pick up tiny insects swarming over the water's surface or even on shoreline plants. In turn, these damselflies are important prey items for birds, frogs, and other insect eaters, including dragonflies.

BROAD-WINGED DAMSELFLIES are large damselflies. All of our species have either partly or wholly *blackish wings* or *clear wings with a spot* at the base of each wing —red in the male and amber in the female. Most species have *metallic body colors,* some very brilliant. They all hunt along streams.

SPREAD-WINGED DAMSELFLIES. No other damselflies hold their wings *half spread* over their bodies when they are at rest. They are *usually metallic green or bronze above* and pale straw color below. All are *clear-winged.* The spread-wings typically inhabit ponds and marshes.

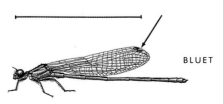

BLUET

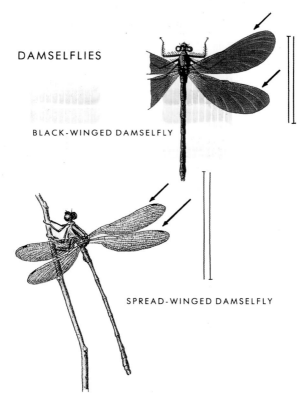

DAMSELFLIES

BLACK-WINGED DAMSELFLY

SPREAD-WINGED DAMSELFLY

GRASSHOPPERS, CRICKETS, MANTIDS, WALKINGSTICKS, AND COCKROACHES.

Most insects in this group are very distinctive, very familiar, or both. You will probably not confuse them with members of other orders. The small, newly hatched nymphs of grasshoppers and crickets might at first be taken for leafhoppers (p. 48) because they jump. But grasshoppers and crickets have very *conspicuous hind legs, usually bent so that the "knee" is held higher than the back;* they also have fairly to very *long antennae, chewing mouth parts,* and a *pair of claspers or "tails"* at the tip of the abdomen. Crickets

23

and cockroaches vaguely resemble beetles, but have membranous wings that do not meet in a line down the center of the back, as the outer wings of beetles do (see p. 56). Beetles also lack "tails."

There are 1015 species of this group in North America. Many species live in grasslands, shrubbery, and treetops. A few are burrowers and some are attracted to human homes. None are aquatic. Most of the species eat plants. Eggs may be attached to or injected into vegetation, deposited in the soil, or simply dropped on the ground. Members of this order undergo simple metamorphosis (see p. 6).

Crickets and grasshoppers are the musical stars of the insect world. They "sing" without the use of voices, however. They produce sounds by rubbing one body part against another, usually a tiny, sharp-edged scraper at the base of one wing over a small, file-like ridge on the underside of the other wing. Males do most of the playing, the main purpose of which is to attract a mate.

SHORT-HORNED GRASSHOPPERS. This group contains our most common grasshoppers. They are active, strong-flying, usually *mottled with brown* or *greenish*, and often occur in large numbers in fields and along roadsides. The family name refers to the antennae, which are relatively *short* and *thick*. One group of short-horned grasshoppers, the band-winged grasshoppers, is characterized by boldly patterned hind wings, sometimes marked with yellow, red, and blue. The "plague locusts" whose ravages are chronicled in the Bible belong to this family. Even in smaller numbers, short-horned grasshoppers are not well liked by farmers. However, these grasshoppers are very important in the diets of birds and other insect-eating animals.

SHORT-HORNED GRASSHOPPERS

antennae relatively short

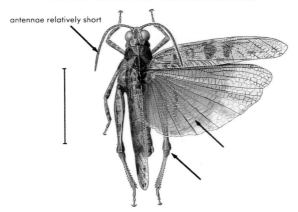

BAND-WINGED GRASSHOPPER

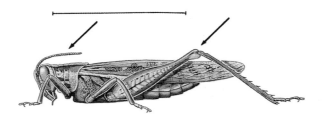

SPUR-THROATED GRASSHOPPER

SLANT-FACED GRASSHOPPER

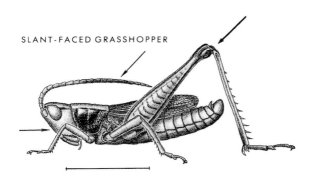

LONG-HORNED GRASSHOPPERS. The best-known member of this family is the Katydid, which "sings" its name from treetops on summer nights. It and most other long-horned grasshoppers are *large, bright green* (rarely brown or even pink), and have *flattened sides.* Their *threadlike antennae* are at least as long as their bodies. The female has an impressive, sword-shaped ovipositor. True Katydids live in trees, but many of their relatives live in fields, wet meadows, shrubs, or weeds. Nymphs and adults generally feed on plants, but some also prey on other insects. They do little damage to cultivated plants.

CAVE OR CAMEL CRICKETS are noticeably *humpbacked, mottled brown* in color, and have very *long antennae.* These crickets inhabit moist, dark places and eat various plants and animals. Wings and sound-producing structures are small or even lacking.

CRICKETS are generally *flat-backed.* Almost all have strong chirping or trilling "songs." They vary in size, form, color, and habits. The blackish Field Crickets that chirp all summer long consist of a number of very similar-looking species. Field Crickets can do serious damage to cultivated plants. They feed by night and eat insects (including each other) as well as plants. Eggs are laid in the ground.

TREE CRICKETS may be the finest of all insect musicians and are much more often heard than seen. Despite the name, some tree crickets live in weedy fields and bushes as well as trees. Tree Crickets lay their eggs in twigs and stems. If you add 40 to the number of chirps the Snowy Tree Cricket gives in 13 or 14 seconds, the total will approximate the temperature in degrees Fahrenheit.

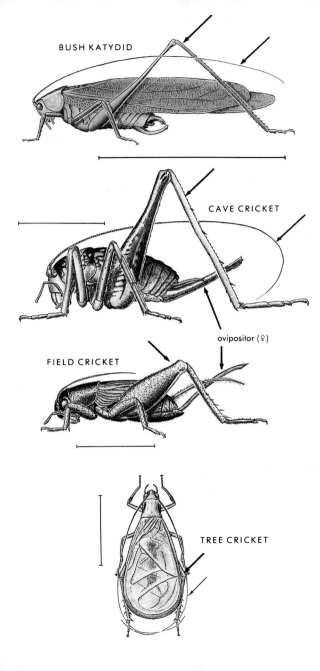

BUSH KATYDID

CAVE CRICKET

ovipositor (♀)

FIELD CRICKET

TREE CRICKET

MANTIDS OR MANTISES are mainly tropical. Three of the 20 North American species were introduced from the Old World. As a mantid waits for an insect or spider to pass within its grasp, it holds its powerful, *clasping forelegs* together, seeming to be rapt in solemn meditation. This posture explains the popular name for this insect— Praying Mantis. Our species are green, gray, or brown, sometimes with yellow markings. Female mantids secrete a foamy mass containing hundreds of eggs. You may find these attached to twigs, where they dry to a tough, paper consistency that lasts through winter. Mantids eat spiders and all kinds of insects, including some beneficial insects such as bees. However, they are generally regarded as effective destroyers of pest insects. Mantids also eat each other at times, but contrary to popular belief, recent research suggests that the female does not eat the male while mating.

WALKINGSTICKS are well named. They are slow-moving insects and their form makes them almost invisible as they eat the leaves of trees and shrubs. If you observe one patiently, you may see it sway gently as it sits, imitating the motion of a twig in the breeze. Eggs are dropped individually on the ground, where they overwinter in leaf litter. Most walkingsticks are tropical.

COCKROACHES are widely known as the rats of the insect world. This bad reputation is based on the few species of cockroaches that scavenge in human habitations. As with many problem species, most of these pests were introduced from other parts of the world. In fact, most cockroach species are tropical, never enter houses, and help the decay process in natural ecosystems. Some cockroaches are even quite handsome. However, the three most common pest species have unwholesome habits, an unpleasant odor, and may occur in large numbers, especially in warmer climates.

Outdoor roaches are usually found in wood-lands under logs or stones; like their relatives that live in houses or other buildings, they feed mainly at night. Many roaches have well-developed wings, but seldom, if ever, fly. Roach egg cases may be cemented in crevices, or the female may carry the capsule on the tip of her abdomen until the nymphs hatch.

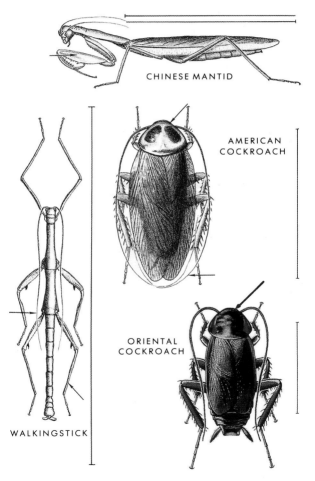

CHINESE MANTID

AMERICAN COCKROACH

ORIENTAL COCKROACH

WALKINGSTICK

TERMITES are *small, soft-bodied,* and usually *pale-colored.* The antennae are relatively *short, straight,* and *threadlike* or *beadlike.* Flying forms have *2 pairs* of wings of *equal length.* The wings are often much longer than the body; however, short-winged forms also occur. Unlike ants, termites never have a constricted "waist" or elbowed antennae.

Termites have sophisticated societies that consist of four or five castes. The members of each caste have specific roles and a corresponding body type. Winged males and females of the reproductive caste are produced in great numbers at a specific time of year (spring for the most common eastern species). These form vast aerial swarms. After mating, pairs shed their wings and disperse to found new colonies. The queens (females of the founding pairs) are comparatively large and long-lived (up to 10 years) and produce most of the colony's eggs. Members of another caste also produce some eggs. The worker caste is made up of sterile (non-breeding) adults and the nymphs of other castes. They are responsible for nest construction, tunneling, and finding food. The soldiers have greatly enlarged jaws, useful for defending the colony, but not for eating food. They are fed by the workers. Some termite species also contain another caste of defensive termites. These termites have a long, slender snout through which they can squirt a sticky liquid at intruders.

Most of the 41 species of North American termites occur in the Southeast. Termites colonize soil or wood. The staple food of termites is the cellulose in wood fiber. Termites are notorious for the damage they do to buildings and other wood products. They also serve a valuable service by breaking down dead wood in forests into soil.

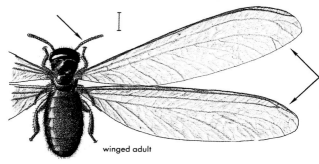

winged adult

TERMITE

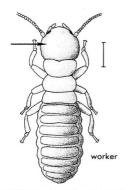

worker

SUBTERRANEAN TERMITE

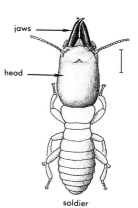

jaws

head

soldier

snout

nasutus

DESERT TERMITE

STONEFLIES. Adult stoneflies are best distinguished from other insects by the combination of two characteristics: a *pair of prominent "tails"* extending from the tip of the abdomen, and *2 pairs of membranous wings* (absent in a few species). The wings are held more or less *flat, overlap* one another over the back, and extend *past the tip of the abdomen.* The soft bodies of stoneflies are usually yellowish, greenish, or some shade of brown. The aquatic nymphs are long and flattened, and lack wings. Like the adults, the nymphs have a pair of "tails," by which you can distinguish them from nymphs of other aquatic insects.

Stonefly nymphs are exceptionally hardy insects and are often the most numerous invertebrates in cold, clean mountain streams. Most stonefly nymphs feed on plant debris and algae, but others are predators of other aquatic insects. They crawl amidst the leaf litter and sediment at the bottom of streams, or cling to the undersides of rocks.

Some adult stoneflies emerge in the middle of winter, finding shelter from extreme cold. Other species appear only in spring, summer, or fall. Despite their long wings, adult stoneflies are weak fliers and spend most of their time resting near the water's edge. Different species become active at different times of day, and some nighttime species are attracted to lights. The shorter-lived species do not feed as adults; others eat foods such as algae, pollen, and plant juices. In some cases male stoneflies attract mates by drumming their abdomens against a resonant surface, such as a hollow log. Eggs are laid on the shore or shallows or dropped in the water.

Stoneflies are a major food source for fish, especially trout. The first known artificial fly was modeled on a British stonefly more than 450 years ago.

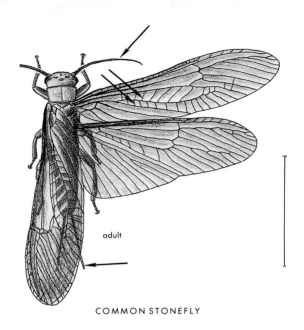

COMMON STONEFLY

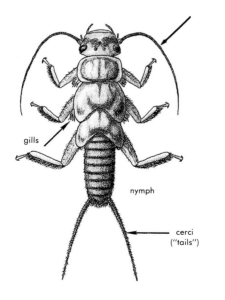

gills

nymph

cerci
("tails")

EARWIGS can be distinguished from all other insects by their *large, hardened "tails,"* which are *shaped like forceps.* Rove beetles (p. 60) are similar, but never have these distinctive "tails." Roaches (p. 28) have long, threadlike antennae.

Earwigs are small to medium-sized (1/8 to 3/4 of an inch long) and brown or blackish in color. Though many species have fully developed wings, earwigs seldom fly. They are scavengers and plant eaters for the most part, active mainly at night. They sometimes feed on cultivated plants. Female earwigs lay their eggs in burrows in the ground or in debris, and guard them until the nymphs hatch. The 18 North American species of earwigs are widespread, and some are abundant.

Earwigs do not (at least as a rule) climb into people's ears. But they can pinch with their "tails" and secrete a pungent liquid if disturbed.

LICE are small or tiny insects, usually less than 3/8 inch long. There are three different orders of lice, which can best be identified by the places where they live and by their feeding habits. Members of one order—booklice—eat starchy material. Chewing lice, which belong to a different order, are parasites on the skin of birds and mammals, but do not attack humans. Sucking lice live on the skin of mammals, and two species—the Crab Louse and Body Louse—attack people. These lice feed on blood, and their bites are often very irritating. They spend their entire life cycle on the host, spreading by contact. Lice can transmit diseases.

The Crab Louse is named for its large claws and general shape. It prefers the human pubic region. There are two forms of the human Body Louse. One lives in the hair of the head, and the other ranges over the entire body and lays its eggs in clothing.

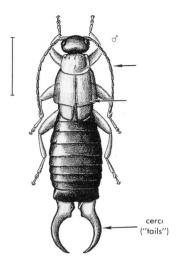

cerci
("tails")

EUROPEAN EARWIG

BOOK LOUSE

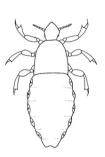

BODY LOUSE

CRAB LOUSE

THRIPS are tiny insects; most are less than
⅙ inch long. They are *long and slim* and
vary in color from pale to blackish. They
have *2 pairs* of *long, narrow* wings (sometimes absent), each fringed with *long hairs.*

Thrips are familiar to most gardeners and
farmers because they are often abundant on
cultivated plants. Thrips damage plants by
sucking plant juices and carrying certain
plant diseases. Some species prey on small
insects, mites, and other invertebrates.
Thrip populations are controlled by other
insects, including ladybird and lacewing
larvae and certain bugs.

BUGS. The forewings of bugs are usually
thickened for most of their length and end
in a *thinner, transparent, membrane-like
tip.* The area where the wings overlap is
usually protected by a *large* and *triangular*
shield. The wings and shield produce a
criss-cross pattern of triangles on the back
that is seen in few other insects. A typical
bug's back is *flat* or gently *rounded* or
humped and is made up of several *distinct
sections* of different textures. Bugs have
sucking mouth parts in the form of a segmented *beak,* folded against the underside
of the body when not in use. Most bugs
have fairly *long, segmented antennae.*
Compare with hoppers (p. 48) and beetles
(p. 56).

The term "bug" is widely used to refer to
all insects or small invertebrates, but ento-
mologists (scientists who study insects)
refer to the members of this order as true
bugs.

There are about 4500 North American
species of bugs. Many species (such as the
Harlequin Bug) are brightly colored, and
either match the plants on which they rest
or stand out from their backgrounds. In the
latter case, the bugs usually taste bad, because
they feed on plants that are poisonous to
other animals. Birds and other predators
learn by experience not to attack these bugs.

Some of our most familiar aquatic insects

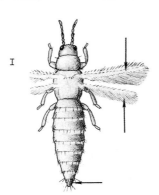

COMMON THRIPS

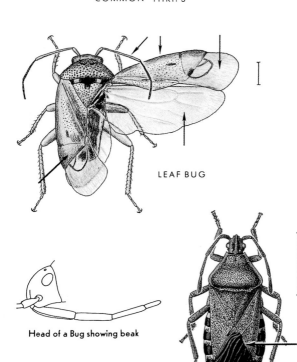

LEAF BUG

Head of a Bug showing beak

SQUASH BUG

belong to this order, though most bugs live on land. The eggs may be inserted into plants, attached to convenient objects, or dropped in the water or on the ground. Some eggs are ornately sculptured or boldly patterned. All bugs undergo simple metamorphosis (see p.6).

Adult bugs live in all imaginable habitats; one group of water striders includes the only insects that live on the open ocean. Most species suck plant juices, and some plant feeders are agricultural pests. Insect control is provided by many other bugs that prey on harmful insects. Many bugs will bite if molested, and a few species suck the blood of mammals, including humans. Diseases are transmitted by certain "kissing bugs," especially in southern climates. Another unpleasant bug trait is the habit of giving off offensive odors to deter enemies.

WATER BOATMEN AND BACKSWIMMERS
are familiar to anyone who has spent time observing pond life. They look quite similar, though they belong to two different families and differ in behavior. Water boatmen swim *right-side-up*, move *erratically*, and spend a lot of time clinging to submerged vegetation. Most feed on algae and tiny aquatic organisms. They do not bite. Backswimmers move *less erratically*, and often rest at the surface in a characteristic position with the *head angling downward* in the water. They eat other aquatic insects, tadpoles, and small fish. Handle backswimmers carefully—their bite is painful. Many members of these families overwinter as adults, and you might see them moving with their distinctive rowing action under the frozen surface of a pond.

HARLEQUIN BUG
(STINK BUG)

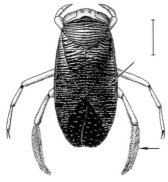

WATER BOATMAN

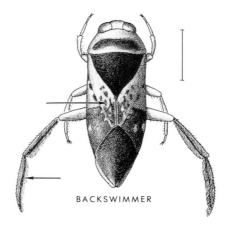

BACKSWIMMER

GIANT WATER BUGS are the largest predatory water bugs. Some tropical species reach a length of more than 4 inches. They are aggressive predators and readily attack fish and frogs as well as other insects. If stepped on by a swimmer, these "toe biters" will deliver a respectable bite, made more painful by the injection of a mild toxin. In some species of giant water bugs, the female glues over a hundred eggs to the back of the male, which carries them around for a week or so until they hatch. These bugs fly well and are strongly attracted to lights. In warm climates where they are most abundant, they sometimes fly onto porches or clatter helplessly over the pavement of lighted parking lots. If handled, they may squeak and give off an apple-like scent. In parts of the Orient, these big bugs are munched like candy bars.

WATER STRIDERS are remarkable for their ability to "skate" over the surface of a pond or a slow-moving stream, poised on segments of their long middle and hind legs. The dense, water-resistant hairs covering the segments at the end of their striding legs trap tiny air bubbles that help keep them afloat. The forelegs are much shorter and are used for grasping insects that fall into the water and, occasionally, aquatic animals that swim close to the surface. Rows of water strider eggs are cemented on floating objects just below the surface. Adults burrow in mud or under stones during the winter or when their habitat dries up temporarily. One group of water striders lives on the surface of the open ocean. None of these attractive insects bite people.

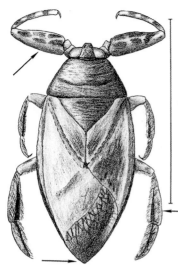

GIANT WATER BUG

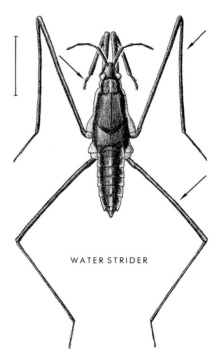

WATER STRIDER

STINK BUGS AND SHIELD-BACKED BUGS.
These are among the most familiar of bugs, and there are many North American species. Look for their broadly *oval shape.* Stink bugs have a large, *triangular* area between the leathery part of the wings. Stink bugs are usually medium-sized and may be dull or brightly colored (see the Harlequin Bug, p. 39). Some species feed on plants, while others prey on moth larvae and other insects. Stink bugs give off *pungent odors* when disturbed. The shield-backed bugs are similar but have a very *broad* shield covering the wings and most of the back, to the tip of the abdomen.

LEAF OR PLANT BUGS. This is the largest family of bugs, containing several hundred North American species. You can recognize them by a *triangular extension* of the thickened part of the forewing. Most species measure less than ⅜ inch long and many are brightly colored. They vary in form. Almost all leaf bugs feed on plants, and some are serious pests.

AMBUSH BUGS are easily recognized by the *flat, skirt-like* extensions at the sides of the abdomen and by their almost grotesquely *enlarged forelegs.* They wear "camouflage" patterns of yellow, green, and brown. These bugs nestle in flowers (especially goldenrod) and suddenly grasp an unsuspecting bee or other insect that has come seeking nectar or pollen.

ASSASSIN BUGS are often of good size and usually brownish or black. They are quite variable in form, but most are a *narrow oval,* sometimes with the *skirt-like extensions* of the abdomen typical of the ambush bugs. Most assassin bugs live on flowers or foliage, but a few species commonly enter houses. These bugs primarily eat other insects, and sometimes bite people.

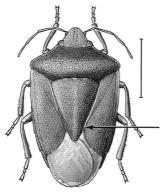

SOUTHERN GREEN STINK BUG

BLOODSUCKING CONENOSE
(ASSASSIN BUG)

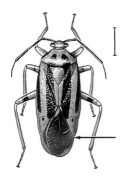

FOUR-LINED
PLANT BUG

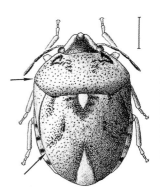

SHIELD-BACKED BUG

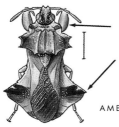

AMBUSH BUG

RED BUGS OR STAINERS are medium-sized to large bugs. Most are *brightly marked* with red, yellow or white. The few North American species live in the southern U.S. One, the Cotton Stainer, is a serious pest. It colors or stains cotton fibers as it feeds, thereby reducing the crop's value. Other stainers feed on oranges, hibiscus, and other plants.

SCENTLESS PLANT BUGS are plant feeders. Most prefer weedy fields. However, one of the most familiar species, the Boxelder Bug, lives in trees. It often enters houses to over-winter. Scentless plant bugs are most common in late summer and early fall. As their name indicates, they do not stink.

SEED BUGS are small to medium-sized and rather variable in shape. Some are brightly colored. One abundant species is the Small Milkweed Bug. Like most members of this large family, it feeds on the mature seeds of its host plant. The Chinch Bug (not illustrated) feeds on the sap of wheat and other grains, and is a serious pest. A few seed bugs feed on insects.

BED BUGS. This is a small but notorious family, the members of which are all less than ½ inch long. The tiny species that sucks human blood lives in creases in mattresses and other cozy niches. It emerges at night, sometimes in small armies, to attack sleeping victims. Fortunately, bed bugs do not carry diseases, but their bites can be very irritating. These bugs thrive in a warm climate.

COTTON STAINER

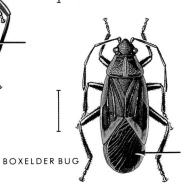

BOXELDER BUG

SMALL MILKWEED BUG

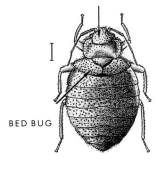

BED BUG

**CICADAS, HOPPERS, APHIDS, AND
SCALE INSECTS.** Most members of this
large and exceptionally varied order are so
distinctive that you are unlikely to mistake
them for other kinds of insects. Some hoppers are similar to certain bugs (p. 36), but
hoppers tend to *fold their wings slanting
down at an angle*, like a tent or roof over
the body, while bugs fold their wings flat
over the back. Because they jump, hoppers
might also be confused with grasshoppers
(p. 23). But hoppers have *sucking mouth
parts* in the form of a *beak*, while grasshoppers have chewing jaws. And the antennae
of hoppers are *short* and *bristle-like*, com-
pared to those of grasshoppers or bugs.

These insects may be tiny or quite large,
dull or brilliantly colored, winged or wingless. Some do not look like insects at all.
Their life histories are also impossible to
stereotype. Females may lay eggs in plants,
drop them on the ground, or bear live
young. Metamorphosis is generally simple
(see p. 6), but there are many variations.
Except for the species that don't feed at all
as adults, all feed on plants. Several groups
contain important agricultural pests. A few
yield products useful to humanity, and
many are quite strange and beautiful.
About 6500 species occur in North America.

CICADAS are best known for their "song" and
their unusual life cycle. Their appearance is
also unique, but because they typically rest
high in trees, you are more likely to hear
them than see them. The *droning, mechan-
ical buzz* produced by males during July
and August is made by vibrating a system of
plates and membranes in a resonating
chamber on the underside of the abdomen.
Cicadas lay their eggs in twigs and plant
stems. The nymphs drop to the ground and
burrow into the soil, where they feed on
roots for two to five years. Because different
broods overlap, some adults appear every
year. The mature nymphs crawl out onto
tree trunks, and the black and green adults

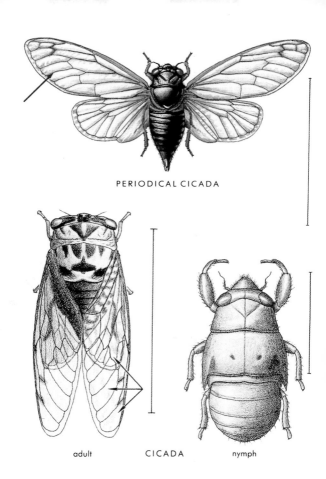

PERIODICAL CICADA

adult   CICADA   nymph

emerge to begin their short lives in trees.
Periodical cicadas (with red eyes and wing
veins) occur in mass emergences every 17
years in the North and every 13 years in the
South. When hordes of these cicadas lay
their eggs, they sometimes damage young
trees. But overall, cicadas are not serious
pests. These insects are popularly called
"locusts," but this name is more correctly
applied to certain grasshoppers (see p. 24).

47

TREEHOPPERS are easily recognized by the unusual shape of their pronotum, which *covers the top of the head* and *extends back* to the tip of the abdomen. This gives these jumping insects a humpbacked appearance. The pronotum may also be shaped to resemble parts of plants, and some treehoppers look exactly like thorns as they cling to woody stems. Most species are less than ½ inch long and are brown or green. Adults feed on plants, but they are not important pests.

FROGHOPPERS, SPITTLEBUGS, AND LEAF-HOPPERS. Adult froghoppers and leafhoppers are very similar. Froghoppers are *squat* and usually *brown* or *green.* Leafhoppers are generally more *slender* and *tapered,* and many are *brightly patterned* in several colors. They are both less than ½ inch long. Froghopper nymphs are aptly called **spittle-bugs.** These hatch on the stems of grasses and other plants. As the nymphs start to feed, they surround themselves with a mass of spittle-like foam, by blowing air bubbles from the tip of the abdomen into a mixture of secretions. Presumably this unique habit keeps the soft-bodied nymphs from drying out and conceals them from predators. There are many species of froghoppers, which feed on a great variety of plants. Many are serious agricultural pests.

PLANTHOPPERS are small jumping insects, up to ⅜ inch long. Many are similar to leafhoppers and froghoppers. They are best distinguished by the location of their antennae: *below* and sometimes *behind* the eyes. Planthoppers lay their eggs in plants, and the nymphs and adults feed on plant juices. This is a large group containing a number of families, but the species are less common on the whole than those of other hoppers, and none are serious pests of cultivated plants.

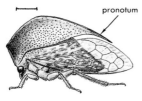
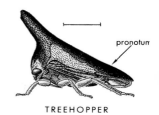

TREEHOPPER

TREEHOPPER

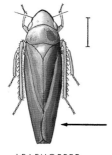

FROGHOPPER

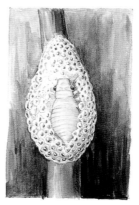

SPITTLEBUG
(FROGHOPPER NYMPH)

inside protective
bubbles

LEAFHOPPER

PLANTHOPPER

PLANTHOPPER

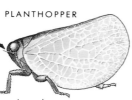

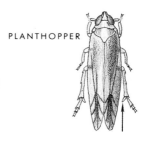

APHIDS OR PLANT LICE. The life cycle of aphids is complex. It typically involves several generations of wingless and winged females, which reproduce without mating, and a generation of both males and females, which mate. The fertilized females lay eggs in bark crevices or near buds. Aphids attack many kinds of plants in.enormous numbers, feeding on all parts. They damage many cultivated plants by feeding on them and by carrying diseases. Fortunately, aphids are eaten by many other insects and birds. As aphids feed, they release excess plant juice and waste products from the tip of the abdomen. This sweet, sticky substance is known as honeydew. It is a food source for some insects. Ants are especially attracted to it, and one species of root-feeding aphid is "domesticated" (protected and "herded") by certain ants for its honeydew.

SCALE INSECTS AND MEALYBUGS. The newly emerged nymph of a scale insect is active, with legs and antennae. In most species, however, these appendages are shed in the next molt, and the insect does not move again. It then feeds on the plant part on which it rests. It produces a *waxy* or *cottony substance*, which is either attached to the body or forms a separate shell over the insect. In its last nymphal stage, the male enters a dormant, non-feeding state similar to a pupa. The adult male emerges with a single pair of wings and resembles a gnat. But unlike a fly, it lacks mouth parts. The adult female remains under the scale and lays its eggs or bears its young there. Scale species come in an extraordinary variety of forms. Some of the soft-bodied scales, such as mealybugs, remain mobile throughout their lives. Many scale insects are serious pests of shade and orchard trees.

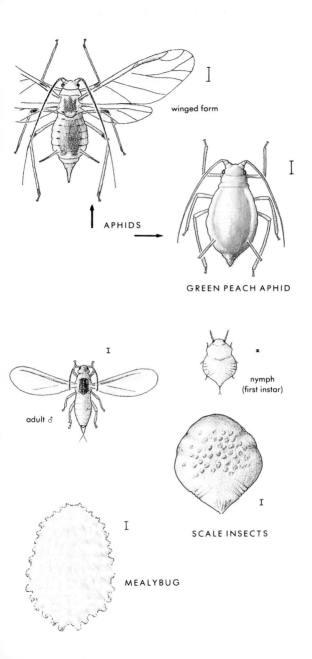

winged form

APHIDS

GREEN PEACH APHID

adult ♂

nymph
(first instar)

SCALE INSECTS

MEALYBUG

DOBSONFLIES, LACEWINGS, AND ANTLIONS.

The members of this order have long, slender bodies and *2 pairs* of equal-sized *membranous,* usually *clear wings,* which they fold like a tent over their bodies when they rest. The membranous wings are reinforced by a lacy network of veins. In most species, the antennae are fairly conspicuous. Dobsonflies might be mistaken for stoneflies (p. 32), but never have the 2 "tails" at the tip of the abdomen that stoneflies always have. Adult antlions resemble damselflies (p. 22), but can always be distinguished by their stout, *clubbed antennae* (damselflies have tiny, bristle-like antennae). Compare members of this order also with caddisflies (p. 73). This is a small group, with only 338 North American species. These insects undergo complete metamorphosis (see p. 7).

DOBSONFLIES. Adult male dobsonflies are among our most bizarre-looking insects. Their wingspan may exceed 6 inches, and their large *crossed jaws* can measure an inch long or more. Though they look fierce, these enlarged jaws are used only to hold the female during mating, and are useless as weapons. The females' much shorter jaws, however, can give a noticeable nip. Adult dobsonflies are active from twilight on, and often flutter awkwardly around house lights. They apparently live for only a few days, and eat little or nothing. Eggs are laid on surfaces that project out over the water. The larvae drop into the water after hatching. They then find shelter under stones and swim or crawl after invertebrate prey, including each other. When mature, the larvae crawl out and pupate. The leggy hellgrammites, as the large dobsonfly larvae are called, are eaten by many freshwater fish and are widely used as bait by anglers.

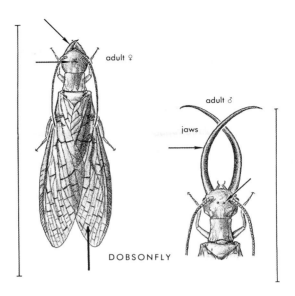

adult ♀

adult ♂

jaws

DOBSONFLY

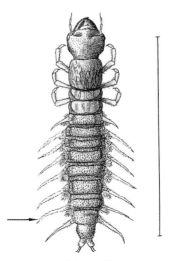

HELLGRAMMITE
(DOBSONFLY LARVA)

LACEWINGS. The most familiar lacewings are *delicate, green* insects with *clear, green-veined* wings, *long* antennae, and bright *golden* eyes. The live in grassy and weedy fields as well as in trees and shrubs, and feed on a variety of small invertebrates. When handled, they give off a strong odor, which has earned them the name "stink-flies." Lacewing larvae are called aphid lions because they feed on aphids (p. 50), and are thus beneficial in controlling these and other plant-eating pests. Some species of lacewing larvae pile empty aphid skins and other debris on their backs, probably as a means of camouflage. Lacewings lay their tiny white eggs atop hairlike stalks, usually on leaves. The larvae pupate in pea-shaped silken cocoons that are hidden in crevices or attached under leaves.

ANTLIONS. With wings outspread, adult antlions resemble weak-flying, gray damsel-flies. But they are easily distinguished by their *clubbed antennae.* You are most likely to see the adults at night, when they are attracted to house lights. Damselflies, in contrast, are active during the day. Little is known of the habits of adult antlions. They are thought to feed on small insects. It is the larvae of these creatures that are the lions. Hatching from eggs that the adults drop on the ground, the odd-looking, bristly larvae dig conical pits in fine, dry earth or sand. They then lie buried at the bottom of the pits, with their jaws poised to catch, paralyze, and suck dry any passing insect—usually an ant—that falls in. The pits often occur in small colonies. The larva eventually spins a silken cocoon with sand woven into the walls, and pupates inside. Antlions are widespread, but more common in the South.

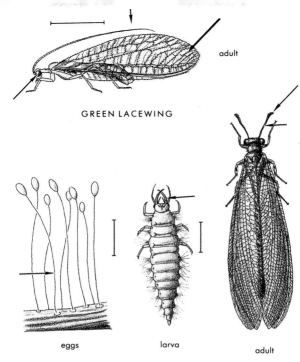

GREEN LACEWING

eggs

larva

adult

ANTLION

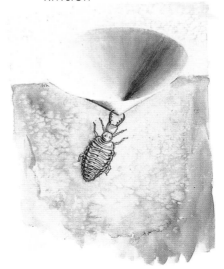

larva with trap

BEETLES can be distinguished by a line that runs *straight* down the *middle of the back.* This marks the place where the 2 hard or leathery wing covers meet. These may be smooth, hairy, grooved, or pitted, but always have the *same texture over their entire surface.* Beetles' flying wings, when present, are usually concealed under the wing covers when the insect is at rest. Beetles also have *chewing jaws.* Beetles undergo complete metamorphosis (see p. 7). The larvae may be wormlike, or resemble a smooth caterpillar, or be fat, soft, and curved—a form called a grub. The pupa resembles a pale, mummified version of the adult beetle. Compare beetles with bugs (p. 36), cockroaches (p. 28), crickets (p. 26), and hoppers (p. 48).

Beetles make up the largest order of living things, with about 290,000 species presently known worldwide. Only 27,000 occur in North America. Beetles are found in almost every habitat and come in all shapes and sizes. In this introductory book, however, there is only room to describe 34 of the 111 families of North American beetles.

TIGER BEETLES are often *colorful,* brilliantly *iridescent,* and *boldly patterned.* You are most likely to see them in open habitats such as beaches, deserts, lake shores, and sunny woodland trails. Speedy predators, tiger beetles chase down other insects on their unusually *long legs.* They take flight when approached. The larvae are also "tigers," and dig holes in the ground, where they wait to seize a passing insect meal in their large jaws. Most of our tiger beetles occur in the West. Handle them carefully— they have an effective bite.

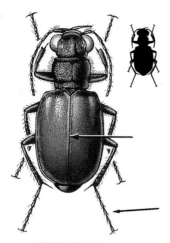

TIGER BEETLE

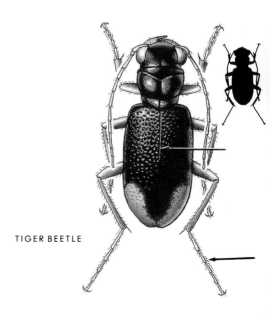

TIGER BEETLE

GROUND BEETLES. This large family contains some of our most abundant beetles. A typical ground beetle is the woodland type. Most species are *black,* but some are *iridescent,* a few spectacularly so. The black species might be mistaken for certain darkling beetles (p. 66), but the form of the antennae will distinguish them in most cases. (To sort out the other look-alikes, you have to count the leg segments under a hand lens or microscope.) Both adults and larvae of ground beetles are, with rare exceptions, predators. They hunt at night and hide under rocks, logs, and other ground cover during the day. The large, colorful *Calosomas* are known as caterpillar hunters and consume great quantities of pests such as cutworms and Gypsy Moth caterpillars. They readily follow their prey into the trees. Ground beetles are common throughout North America.

WATER BEETLES. Members of a number of beetle families are abundant in fresh water, especially where a supply of aquatic plants and invertebrates is available. They range in size from ⅛ to more than 1½ inches long. Most are black, dark brown, or yellowish, and some are patterned lightly in contrasting shades. Water beetles tend to be *streamlined* for efficient movement, and have legs that are modified for swimming. Some are predators, while others are scavengers or graze on water plants. The nymphs are also aquatic in most cases and are important predators.

On a summer day, you may see swarms of whirligig beetles swirling on the surface of a pond or slow river. Perhaps the most interesting feature of these insects is their double eyes, with which they see both above and below the surface. When handled, some species give off an odor of pineapple. Members of other water beetle families, such as the predaceous diving beetles, are less familiar because they live under water.

GROUND BEETLES

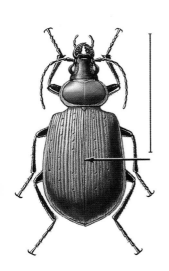

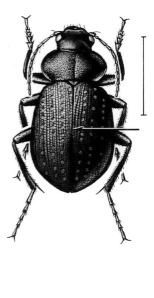

WATER BEETLES

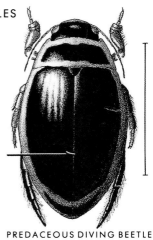

WHIRLIGIG BEETLE

PREDACEOUS DIVING BEETLE

CARRION BEETLES are large, distinctive insects, often marked with *bright splotches* of red or yellow. Some species bury a dead animal and lay their eggs on it, giving the larvae a ready supply of food when they hatch. Adult carrion beetles also visit decomposing carcasses, and are among the most effective natural controls of maggots (fly larvae).

ROVE BEETLES. This is our largest family of beetles, with almost 3100 North American species. You might not recognize them as beetles. Most are *long* and *narrow,* with very *short wing covers* and a number of *exposed abdominal segments,* so that they resemble earwigs (p. 34) without a "tail." Some rove beetles look like roaches (p. 28). Most species are largely brown or black; a few are marked with orange or other bright colors. Most rove beetles eat other insects. Despite their short wing covers, these beetles have fully developed wings and fly well. They often run with the abdomen curled forward like a scorpion's tail. They do not sting, however, although larger species bite.

DERMESTID BEETLES. These small beetles are usually *dull colored* and often *scaly* or *hairy.* The hairy larvae of various species do millions of dollars of damage yearly by eating carpets, silk, fur, leather, upholstery, feathers, stored foods, and museum specimens. Some dermestids also live in bird and insect nests or feed on flowers.

SOFT-WINGED FLOWER BEETLES. This is a fairly large family with a largely western distribution. Its members are common on flowers and are often brightly colored, but you may miss them because of their small size. Adults mainly eat insects, but some eat pollen. The larvae are predators or scavengers.

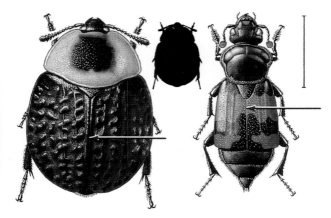

CARRION BEETLES

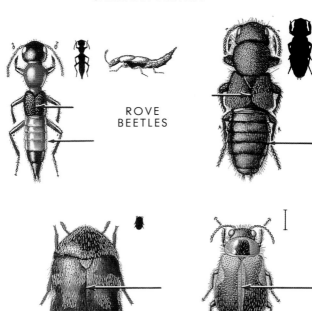

ROVE
BEETLES

DERMESTID BEETLE

SOFT-WINGED
FLOWER BEETLE

LIGHTNINGBUGS OR FIREFLIES are neither bugs nor flies, but soft-bodied beetles. They are typically brown or blackish in color, usually with markings of red or yellow on the *large, shield-like pronotum.* A lightning-bug's most distinctive characteristic is, of course, its light, though not all species have one. It is a cold light produced by chemicals in the firefly's body. Males and females of each species have their own flashing patterns, allowing members of the same species to recognize each other for mating. You may be able to distinguish such patterns as a J, a series of dashes, or a series of dots. Lightningbug larvae feed on slugs, insects, and other invertebrates, and live in damp, swampy habitats. The food eaten by the adults is largely unknown.

NET-WINGED BEETLES. Members of this small family are usually easy to recognize by the unusual form and texture of the wing covers. Most species are patterned in red or yellow and black. Adults of some species of net-winged beetles are known to take live prey; others are apparently scavengers. They are active by day and are fairly common in and near woodlands. The larvae are predators and live under bark.

SOLDIER BEETLES are *long* and *rectangular* in shape. They are *soft-bodied,* usually brown, yellow, or blackish, and have a *prominent,* often brightly colored pronotum. They share these characteristics with many lightningbugs. In soldier beetles, though, the pronotum *never completely covers* the head from above as it always does in the lightningbugs. Adults are common on flowers and leaves. They feed on pollen, nectar, and in some cases small insects such as aphids. Most larvae are predators.

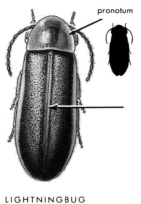

LIGHTNINGBUG
(FIREFLY)

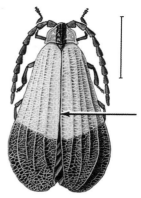

NET-WINGED BEETLE

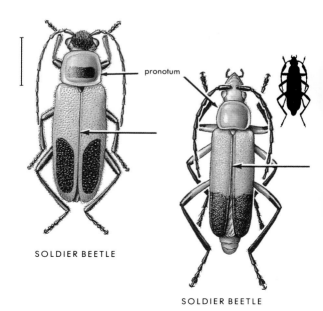

SOLDIER BEETLE

SOLDIER BEETLE

CLICK BEETLES are distinctively *long* and *narrow.* Most species are dull *brown* or *blackish* in color, and only a few are colorful or boldly patterned. A few southern species bear small spots that glow in the dark. This common beetle's most intriguing characteristic is its ability to right itself when it is turned on its back. By means of a small spine on the thorax, it can *flip itself* into the air, with a noticeable *click.* Look for adults on flowers and leaves, under bark, and in rotten wood. Many species apparently do not feed as adults. The larvae, known as wireworms, feed on roots. Several species are agricultural and garden pests.

METALLIC WOOD-BORING BEETLES. Some species in this family look like pieces of colorful metal jewelry because of their *hard, metallic surfaces* and the *sculptured designs* that seem hammered into their wing covers. These beetles somewhat resemble click beetles in shape, but the latter rarely look metallic. The wing covers of many species of wood-boring beetles end in a *double point.* The flat-headed larvae of these beetles are serious pests in orchards and timber stands. The adults eat leaves, bark, and pollen.

BLISTER BEETLES are distinctively shaped with a *broad head, narrow pronotum,* and *loose, leathery wing covers* that curl around the soft abdomen like a stiff cape. Most species of blister beetles are dull, but some are colorfully striped, spotted, or iridescent. The name comes from a burning, oily substance released from the beetles' leg joints as a defense. It is strong enough to blister the skin of humans and animals. The larvae are parasites and transform as they grow, from an active form with legs to a non-active grub. Adults mostly eat plants, and some are pests on crops.

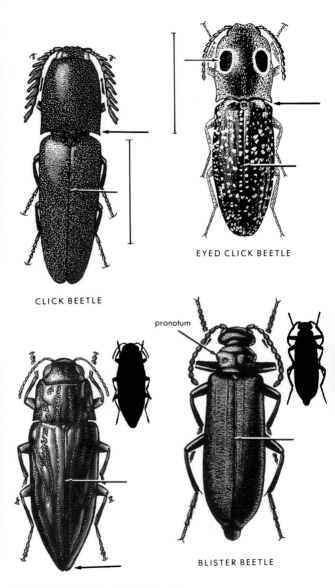

CLICK BEETLE

EYED CLICK BEETLE

pronotum

METALLIC WOOD-BORING BEETLE

BLISTER BEETLE

DARKLING BEETLES. This is a large and varied family, with about 1300 North American species, ranging in size from ⅙ to 1½ inches. Most are dull black or brown in color. Many darkling beetles closely resemble ground beetles (p. 56), some look like leaf beetles (p. 70), and some almost defy description. The adults live on the ground, under bark, in rotten wood, in fungi, and in ant and termite nests. Both adults and larvae of most species are scavengers on decaying plants and animals. A few eat living roots, tubers, or flowers. The most serious pests among these beetles are the mealworms that infest stored grain. Only a little over ¹⁄₁₀ of the North American species of darkling beetles occur in the East. Darkling beetles are common in dry habitats in the West and are active mainly at night. One group of western darklings is noted for its mass migrations in spring.

STAG BEETLES are named for the males of certain species, which have very *long, pronged jaws.* Females and males with smaller jaws can usually be distinguished from similar beetles by their *elbowed antennae.* All are black to reddish brown in color. The Giant Stag Beetle of the Southeast is a formidable creature nearly 2½ inches long, bearing imposing "antlers." When disturbed, some species make themselves look even more fierce by rearing up and opening their jaws. This is a bluff, however, as they are capable only of a weak pinch. Males of some species have been reported to "lock horns" in competition for a mate. Stag beetle larvae live in decaying logs and stumps. Adults are thought to feed mainly on honeydew and sap from leaves and trees. Most of the 30 North American species are woodland insects. Stag beetles are not very common, but gather in some numbers near lights.

DARKLING BEETLE

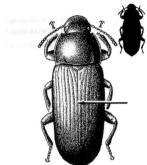

YELLOW MEALWORM
(DARKLING BEETLE)

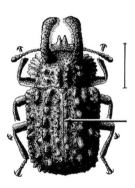

FORKED FUNGUS BEETLE
(DARKLING BEETLE)

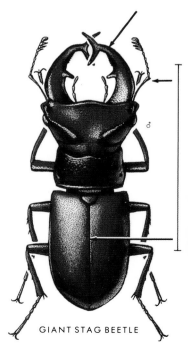

GIANT STAG BEETLE

SCARAB BEETLES. This is one of the largest families of beetles, with some 1300 North American species. The typical scarab is a *stout, heavy-bodied* beetle. Many species are *brilliantly colored. Horns* on the head, pronotum, or both are common. Several well-known groups of scarabs are described below.

DUNG BEETLES. Several groups of scarabs dispose of dung, carrion, and other organic wastes. Perhaps the best known of these are the "tumblebugs," which roll pieces of dung into balls as large or larger than themselves. The female lays eggs in the ball, and then buries it to supply food for the emerging larvae. The ancient Egyptians associated the sphere of dung with the sun, and these beetles were thus considered sacred.

JUNE BEETLES AND CHAFERS. More than a third of our scarabs belong to this group. Many are agricultural or garden pests. The larvae typically eat roots of grasses and other crops. The adults eat leaves and fruit. Most "junebugs" feed at night and often buzz noisily around house lights.

SHINING LEAF CHAFERS are often extraordinarily beautiful, but are also often very destructive, both as larvae and adults. Few of us can appreciate the color pattern of the Japanese Beetle as it munches through a rose bush or an orchard. Its larvae, like others in this group, eat roots and are especially destructive to lawns.

RHINOCEROS, ELEPHANT, AND HERCULES BEETLES are often *large* and *horned,* as their names imply. Tropical members of this group are among the largest insects in the world. The larvae eat roots or decaying wood; adults prefer leaves. Some species damage crops.

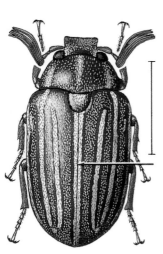

TENLINED JUNE BEETLE

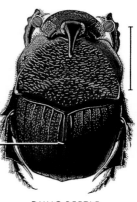

DUNG BEETLE

SCARAB
BEETLES

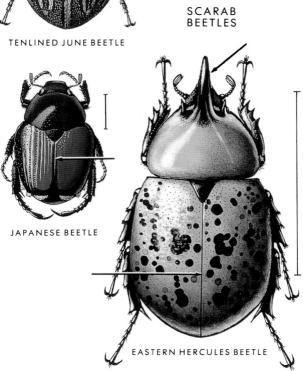

JAPANESE BEETLE

EASTERN HERCULES BEETLE

LONG-HORNED BEETLES are very popular with collectors because of their striking color patterns and great diversity (1100 North American species). Their "horns," actually their antennae, are almost always at least *half as long* as the body—sometimes *twice as long.* Both adults and larvae feed exclusively on plants. The larvae, called round-headed borers, damage much lumber, by chewing their way through it after it has been felled but before it is sawed. They are beneficial, however, in helping fallen trees or limbs decompose in forests. Adult long-horned beetles feed on pollen, nectar, bark, leaves, sap, fruit, roots, and fungi. You are most likely to see them on flowers, where they help spread pollen, as bees do. Handle longhorns carefully: they bite!

LADY OR LADYBIRD BEETLES are familiar to everyone as "ladybugs." Their popularity is well deserved, as they are among the most helpful insects. Of the 400 North American species, only 3 feed on plants. Most of the rest devour vast quantities of agricultural pests such as aphids and scale insects. They are released by the thousands in crop fields and orchards. Both adults and larvae are predators, and they will eat all stages of soft-bodied insects. The name originated in the Middle Ages, when these beetles were associated with the Virgin Mary.

LEAF BEETLES. This is another very large and varied family, with 1474 North American species. Few are more than ½ inch long, and many are *brightly colored.* Most leaf beetles feed on non-woody plants, the larvae eating roots and the adults leaves. Gardeners and farmers are all too familiar with the names of many members of this family.

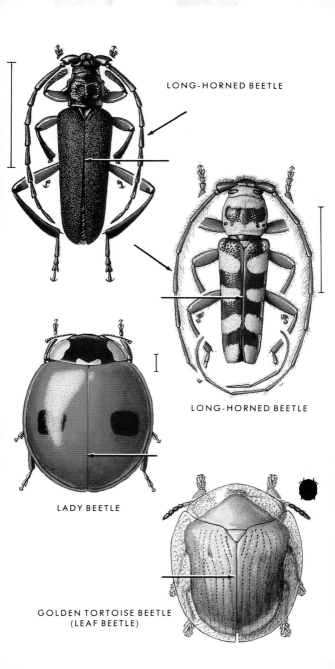

LONG-HORNED BEETLE

LONG-HORNED BEETLE

LADY BEETLE

GOLDEN TORTOISE BEETLE
(LEAF BEETLE)

SNOUT BEETLES OR WEEVILS. There are more than 2400 species of weevils in North America. You can recognize most weevils by their *long*—sometimes very long—*beaks* or snouts. Most species are *small* and *brown or gray.* They are often *hairy* or covered with *tiny scales.* All of our species are plant feeders, and some are serious pests. The larvae feed on all parts of plants, mainly inside buds, twigs, seedpods, fruit, or nuts. Adults tend to eat leaves, pollen, flowers, fruit, or fungi. Most weevils prefer young, rapidly growing plants as well as those in flower or in fruit, and they tend to be most common in wet areas. Many are active at night. In some groups of snout beetles the

SNOUT BEETLES
(WEEVILS)

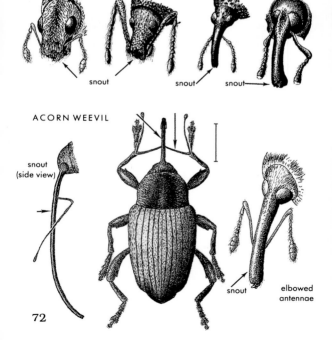

snout

snout

snout

ACORN WEEVIL

snout
(side view)

snout

elbowed
antennae

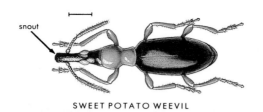

snout

SWEET POTATO WEEVIL

females reproduce without being fertilized, and in fact no males are known for these species.

CADDISFLIES are *small* to *medium-sized, dull-colored* insects with *long, threadlike antennae* and *2 pairs* of *hairy wings* that are held like a tent over the body when they rest. They look like moths, and are attracted to lights. But they have *chewing mouth parts,* instead of the coiled mouth parts of moths. And the wings are never covered with powdery scales as is typical of moths.

Caddisflies are active mainly at night. You might see them whirling in great numbers around street lights or clinging to porch screens. Their days are spent mainly resting in the shade near the stream or pond from which they emerged. As adults, caddisflies seem to spend little time feeding, though some are known to sponge up plant juices and other liquids. Before mating, some species gather in courtship swarms. They lay eggs in masses or strings, usually on stones or other objects in the water.

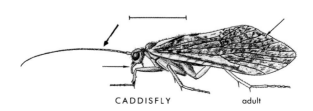

CADDISFLY   adult

73

Though some species spend their larval stage looking like aquatic caterpillars, most construct a protective shelter of pebbles, twigs, and bits of leaves, and so are known as "casebearers." These little shelters come in a variety of designs, each species having its own distinctive style. The larva binds the building materials in a cocoon of silk. Most caddisfly larvae feed on algae and other plants. However, the larvae that make no cases are usually predators or scavengers.

When the larvae are mature, casebearing species anchor their cases to something on the bottom and pupate within them, covering the entrance with a cap of silk or debris. The free-living larvae spin a cocoon. The pupae remain active, and when they are ready, they chew their way out of their cases, crawl out on shore or up an object sticking out of the water, and molt into adult caddisflies. These insects are an important food source for fish and other aquatic animals. A number of species are models for trout flies. Caddisflies occur throughout North America, wherever there is fresh water.

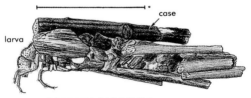

NORTHERN CADDISFLY

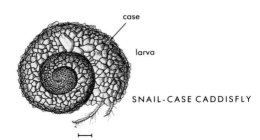

SNAIL-CASE CADDISFLY

BUTTERFLIES AND MOTHS. Taken as a whole, these are the most distinctive of insects. A few moths have wingless forms or mimic other kinds of insects (see p. 92), and these might cause confusion at first. But any insect with *2 pairs of wings,* thickly —often beautifully—covered with layers of *fine, powdery scales* is bound to be a butterfly or moth. Butterflies and moths are also the only insects with sucking mouth parts in the form of a *coiled tube.* Caddisflies (p. 73) are similar but lack coiled mouth parts.

This order is second only to the beetles in size, with 112,000 species worldwide. We tend to be more aware of butterflies, probably because they are often large and colorful and fly in daylight. But of the 11,000 North American species in this order, all but about 700 species are moths. Larvae, known as caterpillars, may be smooth or densely hairy, drab or brilliantly patterned. Some have horns or fake "eyes." A few have stinging hairs or spines, and some give off an unpleasant odor when molested, but most are harmless.

CATERPILLARS
(BUTTERFLY LARVAE)

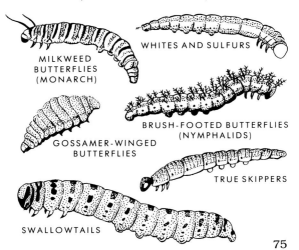

MILKWEED
BUTTERFLIES
(MONARCH)

WHITES AND SULFURS

BRUSH-FOOTED BUTTERFLIES
(NYMPHALIDS)

GOSSAMER-WINGED
BUTTERFLIES

TRUE SKIPPERS

SWALLOWTAILS

The pupal stage of a butterfly, called a chrysalis (plural: chrysalids), often has small points, knobs, or other projections. It is usually attached to the larval food plant by a silk thread spun from the mouth of the caterpillar. Pupae of moths and skippers (see p. 84) are typically smooth and capsule-shaped. In many species of moths, the larva spins a cocoon around the pupa for added protection. Moth cocoons and pupae may be attached to plants, lie on the ground under leaf litter, or rest underground.

In the larval stage, most butterfly and moth species feed on leaves, often of a particular plant or related group of plants. Some bore into leaves, stems, or fruit; a few make galls on living plants; and a very few prey on other insects. Some butterflies and many more moths are serious household, garden, agricultural, or timber pests. Adult butterflies feed mainly on nectar from flowers, but many also feed on sap from plant wounds or on fluids obtained from carrion and dung. Relatively little is known about what different species of moths eat as adults. Some eat nectar and sap. Others live only a short time as adults and do not feed at all. Wherever there are larval food plants and nectar sources for adults there are bound to be butterflies and moths.

SWALLOWTAILS. This family contains the world's largest and most gorgeous butterflies. Most adult swallowtails prefer open country, but a few favor woodland trails and margins. Most swallowtail larvae are *colorfully marked.* These caterpillars feed on leaves of a wide variety of trees and nonwoody plants, and some are pests. Swallowtails range throughout North America, except for the highest reaches of the Arctic. Most species occur in the South and West.

CHRYSALIDS
(BUTTERFLY PUPAE)

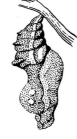

TRUE SKIPPERS

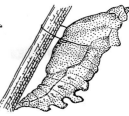

SWALLOWTAILS

**BRUSH-FOOTED BUTTERFLIES
(NYMPHALIDS)**

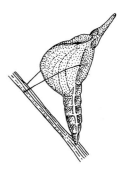

**GOSSAMER-WINGED
BUTTERFLIES**

WHITES AND SULFURS

SWALLOWTAILS

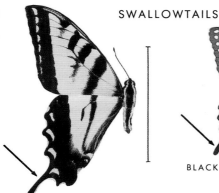

WESTERN TIGER SWALLOWTAIL

BLACK SWALLOWTAIL

WHITES AND SULFURS. Most of the common species in this family prefer open habitats, and it is not unusual to find 3 or more species flying together over a meadow. You may also find these and certain other butterflies gathered in flocks at the edges of mud puddles. The purpose of this behavior is not well understood. The larvae of this group eat various mustards, heaths, willows, and clovers. The Cabbage Butterfly, introduced from Europe, is a pest of cabbage, and some sulfurs occasionally damage alfalfa and clover crops.

GOSSAMER-WINGED BUTTERFLIES. Except for their *small size,* many members of this large family appear to have little in common, but all share traits that other butterflies lack. The caterpillars often look like slugs: *compact, flattened* above, and *tapered* at both ends. In a number of species, the larvae have a mutually beneficial relationship with ants. They secrete a sweet liquid from a gland on the back, which the ants eat. The ants in turn may protect the larvae from parasitic wasps. Larvae in this family also eat the leaves of a wide variety of plants, as well as some fruits.

Coppers are very active. You may see males darting out from flower perches in pursuit of a mate. The larvae eat dock. Many species of blues seem truly gossamer-winged, so fine is the *azure sheen* they exhibit from above. Two of our species, called pygmy blues, are the smallest of all butterflies. Their wing spans are less than $3/8$ of an inch. Some blues live on mountaintops and in the Arctic. Most North American species occur in the West. Hairstreaks are usually *brown* or *gray;* the species are hard to identify. They usually have one or more *"tails"* projecting from the rear edge of the hind wings, and *spots* of orange and blue near the tails on the underside.

WHITES AND
SULFURS

CABBAGE BUTTERFLY

ORANGE SULFUR

AMERICAN COPPER

GOSSAMER-
WINGED
BUTTERFLIES

SPRING AZURE

COMMON HAIRSTREAK

BRUSH-FOOTED BUTTERFLIES OR NYM-PHALIDS. This is the largest family of butterflies, excepting the skippers (p. 84). It contains many of our most familiar species. The name "brush-footed" refers to the front legs of these butterflies, which are very *short* and *hairy* and useless for walking.

The Great Spangled Fritillary is typical of its group, though many are much smaller. The showy *silver "spangles"* on the undersides of the wings are a common characteristic. Leaves of violets are the preferred food of most fritillary larvae. The larvae are *spiny* and in many cases feed only at night.

Checkerspots are among the smaller nymphalids and often bear spectacular color patterns of *red, black,* and *white.* The larvae eat a wide range of plants.

In anglewings, admirals, painted ladies, and related species, the *outer edges* of the wings are *angular.* Most species have an *orange and black pattern* on the upperside of the wings. When anglewings rest on trees with their wings closed, the bright upperwing pattern is largely concealed and the dull, mottled underwing pattern blends with the tree bark. Most species live in temperate forests and hibernate as adults in tree crevices, building eaves, and similar shelters. The Mourning Cloak emerges very early from its winter roost, and can sometimes be seen flying over the snow. A few species in this group, such as the Painted Lady (not shown), are migratory. In general, anglewings prefer to feed on flowing sap or rotting fruit, rather than at flowers. The larvae are *spiny;* they eat the leaves of nettle, elm, birch, willow, hops, and flowers in the composite (daisy) family.

BRUSH-FOOTED BUTTERFLIES

GREAT SPANGLED FRITILLARY

SILVERY CHECKERSPOT

MOURNING CLOAK

RED ADMIRAL

NYMPHS AND SATYRS are all small to medium-sized butterflies, generally *brown* or *gray* in color. A number of species have patches of tawny or reddish, and most are marked above and below with prominent *eyespots*. As the species names imply, many wood nymphs and satyrs are woodland insects, though the Wood Nymph and some others fly mainly over meadows or marshes. These butterflies feed on rotten fruit, sap, or dung, rather than at flowers. The *green*, usually *striped* larvae are *tapered* at both ends and the abdomen has a *forked tip*. They feed at night on grasses and sedges.

MILKWEED BUTTERFLIES. Only 3 members of this family occur in North America. One of them, the Monarch, is a butterfly that nearly everyone knows. It is a large and showy species, abundant throughout most of North America. The large, *tiger-striped* caterpillar feeds only on milkweeds. As it feeds, the caterpillar absorbs a poison from the milkweed. The poison is not harmful to the caterpillar, but when birds and other predators eat a Monarch caterpillar or adult, they become violently ill. Predators thus learn to avoid the striped caterpillars and distinctive orange and black adults. The Viceroy, which belongs to a different family (brush-footed butterflies, p. 80), has evolved coloring that closely mimics that of the Monarch. It, too, is avoided by predators, even though it will not make them sick.

Monarchs migrate hundreds or thousands of miles south for the winter. Some roost in Florida or California, but tens of millions of monarchs overwinter in a mountain forest in central Mexico. In the spring, the Monarchs start back north, laying eggs along the way. The butterflies produced from these eggs continue north. They reach the northernmost fields where milkweeds grow in time to lay the eggs that will become the next generation, which will migrate south in the fall.

WOOD NYMPH

MONARCH
(MILKWEED BUTTERFLY)

VICEROY
(BRUSH-FOOTED
BUTTERFLY)

SKIPPERS are usually classified between the butterflies and moths, and show characteristics of both groups. They also show some uniquely their own, such as *hooked antennae*. The most familiar skippers are generally *small* and *dull*, though quite a few are *tawny yellow*, marked with *silver*, or both. Many species are very similar and difficult to distinguish from one another. As their name implies, they are fast fliers. Skipper larvae have a notable *large head*, with the front of the thorax appearing to be a *"neck."* They feed at night and rest during the day in a rolled leaf that they fasten with silk. Caterpillars of most North American species eat grasses and leaves of the pea family. Pupation occurs in a loose cocoon of dead leaves and silk. Well over 200 species of skippers occur throughout North America.

SPHINX OR HAWK MOTHS are medium-sized to large moths with notably *fat bodies* and unusually *narrow wings.* The clear-winged sphinxes that feed by day are often mistaken for hummingbirds as they dart from flower to flower, their wings blurred by speed. Most hawk moths fly at dusk or at night. Almost all sphinx larvae have a *soft, harmless spine* at the tip of the abdomen and are sometimes called **hornworms.** When disturbed, a hornworm sometimes rears up in a threatening posture that apparently reminded some romantic entomologist of the great Sphinx in Egypt. You may see one of these caterpillars or hornworms covered with white lumps that look like grains of rice. These are the pupae (cocoons) of braconid wasps (see p. 108). The larvae of these wasps parasitize and kill the hornworm. The larvae of most sphinx moths pupate underground.

SILVER-SPOTTED SKIPPER

SKIPPERS

ARCTIC SKIPPER

COMMON CHECKERED
SKIPPER

SPHINX
OR
HAWK
MOTHS

WHITE-LINED SPHINX MOTH

CLEAR-WINGED SPHINX MOTH

GIANT SILKWORM OR SATURNID MOTHS.
This family contains some of the largest and
most beautiful insects in the world. Many of
them have large *"eyespots"* on their wings,
which are believed to surprise or alarm
potential predators. Males have unusually
broad, featherlike antennae. They find
mates by "smelling" a chemical attractant
that the females release into the night air.
Saturnids lack functional mouth parts and
do not feed as adults. Some species, especially males, are active by day. Others are
active at night and are attracted to lights.
Many of the larvae are impressive, often
bearing colorful *stripes, spots,* and *horns.*
Some larvae in this group also bear *stinging
spines.* Saturnid larvae eat a wide variety of
leaves, mainly of trees and shrubs. Most
species spin a silk cocoon in which they
pupate, sometimes incorporating leaves for
camouflage. The silkworm moth on which
the commercial silk trade is based belongs
to a different family and is not native to
North America.

GEOMETERS. In many of these moths the
wings are *sharply angular, brightly colored*
(especially in yellow), and *boldly patterned.*
Geometers typically rest with their *wings
spread flat,* and you are likely to see them
during the day. Females of a few species are
wingless. The name, meaning "earth mea-
surer," refers to the larvae, which are called
inchworms, spanworms, measuring worms,
and loopers. All of these names describe
their distinctive "stride," in which the front
of the body is extended and the rear
brought up to meet it, making an arch or
loop in the middle. These caterpillars feed
on a wide variety of plants, and the famly
contains a number of orchard and shade
tree pests. Geometers are common nearly
everywhere.

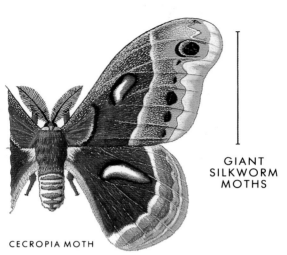

GIANT
SILKWORM
MOTHS

CECROPIA MOTH

IO MOTH

NOTCH-WINGED GEOMETER MOTH

larva
(inchworm)

TENT CATERPILLARS. Most of the members of this small family neither make tents nor do any harm. The group is named mainly for the Eastern Tent Caterpillar. As you have probably seen, this species can defoliate an entire tree in a few weeks. It frequently attacks apple and cherry trees. The larvae hatch in the spring and begin to spin their silken tents, usually in the crotches of trees. They feed outside the tents, which are used only for shelter. The larvae become mature by late May or early June, and pupate in a cocoon attached in a protected spot. The adults emerge in about 3 weeks, mate, and lay masses of eggs aroung twigs of their food trees. These are "varnished" to protect them over the winter. Compare Fall Webworms (below) and Gypsy Moths (p. 90).

TIGER MOTHS. These are some of our most beautiful moths. Because tiger moths are active at night, you are most likely to see them around your house lights. Tiger moth caterpillars are usually very *bristly*, and when molested they often *curl up in a ball.* The most familiar of these, active during the day, are the woolly bears. The amount of black on the Banded Woolly Bear (the caterpillar of the Isabella Tiger Moth) is mistakenly thought by some to predict the severity of the coming winter.

Most tiger moth larvae feed on grasses. A few eat lichens, and several do serious damage to trees and shrubs. The worst of these is the Fall Webworm, which hatches in late summer and fall. Unlike tent caterpillars, these larvae make tents around leaves, sometimes covering whole branches in sheets of silk. They feed on a great variety of plants, often reducing the leaves to mere "skeletons."

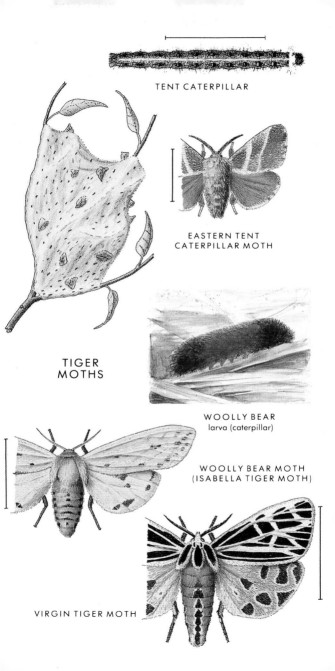

TENT CATERPILLAR

EASTERN TENT
CATERPILLAR MOTH

TIGER
MOTHS

WOOLLY BEAR
larva (caterpillar)

WOOLLY BEAR MOTH
(ISABELLA TIGER MOTH)

VIRGIN TIGER MOTH

NOCTUIDS. This is by far the largest family of moths, with over 2700 species known to occur in North America. Most of the *medium-sized, brown* or *gray* moths that fly in swarms around lights are likely to be noctuids. The glamorous members of the family are the underwings, most of which are fairly large and have striking patterns on the hind wings, in *black* with *red, yellow,* or *white.* Most noctuid moths are active at night. Some adults are known to feed on sap and nectar. Noctuid larvae feed on virtually everything, and a number of species, notably the cutworms, armyworms, and loopers, sometimes harm crops and trees. Some species pupate in a cocoon above ground, others inside their food plants or in the soil, with no other protection.

TUSSOCK MOTHS. Many members of this family cause serious damage to timber, fruit, and shade trees. The group's name comes from *white tufts of hair,* resembling tiny shaving brushes that sit in a row on the back of the mature larva. These and other body hairs can cause an irritating skin rash, if you handle the larva. At present, our worst tussock moth pest is the Gypsy Moth, a native of Europe introduced into Massachusetts in 1866. The larvae usually feed on oak leaves, but will also eat the leaves of many other tree species, including conifers. Gypsy Moth caterpillars may defoliate vast areas of forest within a few weeks, and if they also strip trees of their second growth of leaves, many of the trees may die. Gypsy Moth outbreaks occur in cycles of 8–9 years. The outbreaks run their course naturally in 1–2 years, causing little long-term harm and possibly some benefits.

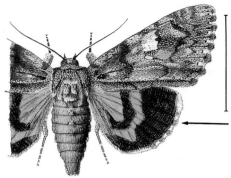

ILIA UNDERWING

NOCTUIDS

EIGHT-SPOTTED FORESTER

CABBAGE LOOPER MOTH

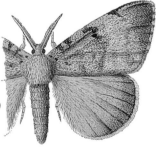

GYPSY MOTH
(TUSSOCK MOTH)
♂

GYPSY MOTH
larva (caterpillar)

PYRALID OR SNOUT MOTHS. This is one of the largest families of moths, with over 1100 species in North America. They are *small to medium-sized* and the species vary widely in form and color pattern. You can recognize most by a projection of the mouth parts that resembles a *snout.* In one group of common species, the moths hold their wings closely *rolled around the body* when they are at rest. Many pyralid larvae feed on leaves when young, and become stem borers when they are older. Many others feed on grass and other roots, and a few are aquatic. Of the many pest species in this group, the best known is probably the European Corn Borer. Others damage pine trees and stored grains.

CLOTHES AND CARPET MOTHS belong to a family of about 180 *small, plain* moths, most of which are scavengers or feed on fungi. Few eat leaves. Three species feed on fabrics, especially woollens. One of these makes silken galleries in the cloth on which it feeds. Much of the fabric damage attributed to moths is really the work of dermestid beetles (see p. 60).

CLEAR-WINGED MOTHS have evolved forms that *mimic wasps.* These moths feed at flowers in the daytime. They typically *lack scales* over much of their wing surfaces, and are *brightly colored,* like the insects they have come to resemble. The larvae bore into roots, stems, and bark. The Peach-tree Borer is one of the few pests among the 125 North American species.

CTENUCHIDS, unlike most other moths (except the sphinx moths, p. 84), feed on flowers during the daytime. A number of species *resemble wasps.* These species have *dark wings,* sometimes with yellow, bright *metallic blue bodies,* and *spots* of yellow or red. Most ctenuchid larvae feed on grasses.

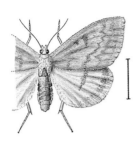

EUROPEAN CORN
BORER MOTH

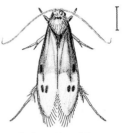

CLOTHES MOTH

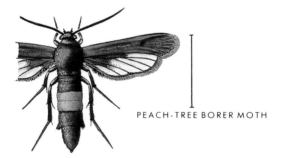

PEACH-TREE BORER MOTH

VIRGINIA CTENUCHA

FLIES have a *single pair* of *transparent wings* (sometimes smoky or patterned), and this feature alone will distinguish them from all similiar insects except for a very few uncommon forms. Most flies also have a relatively *soft body* and *short, bristle-like antennae.* Many flies mimic bees and wasps, both in appearance and behavior, and you might thus be confused between the two at times. But all bees and wasps have *2 pairs* of wings, and most have relatively *long antennae.*

To most people, the word "fly" suggests something obnoxious. However, few species of flies are pests. Many flies are beneficial, fascinating in their habits, and quite beautiful. This is the fourth largest insect order worldwide, and the third largest in North America, with over 16,000 species.

The typical fly larva, called a maggot, is wormlike, with *no legs* and a *poorly developed head.* The larvae of many fly species are aquatic. These usually eat decaying plant matter or catch prey. Other fly larvae live in the soil, in decaying wood, in dung and carrion, or are parasites on other animals. A few eat plants. Flies undergo complete metamorphosis (see p. 7), usually pupating in or near the larval habitat.

All adult flies have *sucking mouth parts,* but this by no means limits their ways of life. Some species are aggressive predators that seize other insects or spiders and suck out their body juices. Others use their mouth parts to take in nectar from flowers. Some flies do not feed at all as adults.

Fly larvae (maggots) are beneficial in disposing of carrion and animal wastes, and many adult flies prey on or parasitize pest insects or pollinate plants. Even the bothersome species are an important source of food for other animals, especially birds.

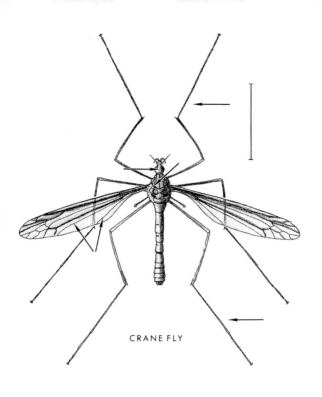

CRANE FLY

CRANE FLIES are distinctive insects with *long, narrow wings* and very *long, fragile legs.* Most are *brown* or *gray,* and some species have *smoky* or *patterned wings.* Crane fly larvae live in water or moist soil and feed on decaying plants. Adults frequent waterside plants and are often attracted to lights. Many species apparently do not feed at all as adults, though some are found on flowers and a few may catch prey. Though they look like large mosquitoes, crane flies do not bite. There are nearly 1500 North American species of crane flies.

MOSQUITOES are all too familiar to most people. They lay their eggs singly or in rafts on the surface of water. They prefer small, still bodies of water. In fact, some species breed only in temporary sites such as tree holes, tin cans, or other places where rain water collects. The larvae, sometimes called "wrigglers," live near the surface of the water in most cases, breathing through a tiny tube at the tip of the abdomen. Most feed on organic debris and algae, but a few eat other mosquito larvae and similar live prey. The pupae, also aquatic, are very active and are sometimes called "tumblers" because of their characteristic movements. Adult mosquitoes of most species are active mainly at night and near dawn and dusk. During the day they roost in shady, sheltered spots. Only the females bite. The males eat nectar and other plant juices. Before a mosquito can siphon up blood, she must dilute it with her saliva. The saliva causes the bite to itch, and also transmits diseases such as yellow fever, malaria, and encephalitis. There are about 150 North American species of mosquitoes, many of them locally or seasonally very abundant. Very few transmit disease.

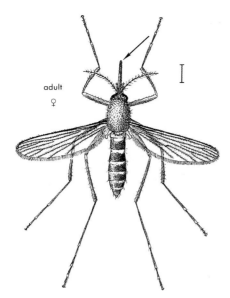

adult
♀

MOSQUITOES

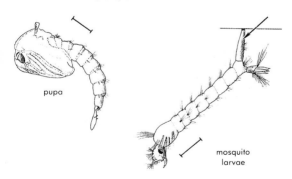

pupa

mosquito
larvae

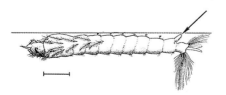

MIDGES closely resemble mosquitoes, but do not bite. They usually occur near ponds and lakes, sometimes in huge, dense swarms that can be seen and heard from a surprising distance. The larvae of most species live in fresh water; a few live in the soil or under bark. Midges are important chiefly as food for other animals.

BITING MIDGES, also known as punkies or no-see-ums, are tiny flies often less than ⅛ inch in length. The species that bite can be extremely bothersome. They tend to swarm on beaches and along river and lake shores, especially around dawn and dusk. The larvae are *long* and *slender*, and live in water or damp situations such as mud, sand, or decaying plants. Adult punkies also attack other insects.

BLACK FLIES are often abundant near rivers and streams in the north woods. The females are vicious biters. Larvae hold on to rocks in running water. Pupation takes place within a silken cocoon, also attached under water. The adult emerges in an air bubble, in which it rises to the surface. Black flies can occur in such vast numbers that livestock have died of shock or blood loss from their bites.

HORSE FLIES OR TABANIDS. These *medium-sized to large* flies are well known for their painful bite. Adults are usually *dull colored* (some are yellow) except for the eyes, which are often *bright green* or *striped* with rainbow iridescence. Various biting species are known as deer flies, greenheads, or horse flies. Only the females feed on blood. They lay eggs in water or on nearby plants. The larvae are mostly aquatic and prey on other insect larvae, worms, and snails. Adult tabanids typically swarm around marshes and other wetlands, but many occur in woodlands.

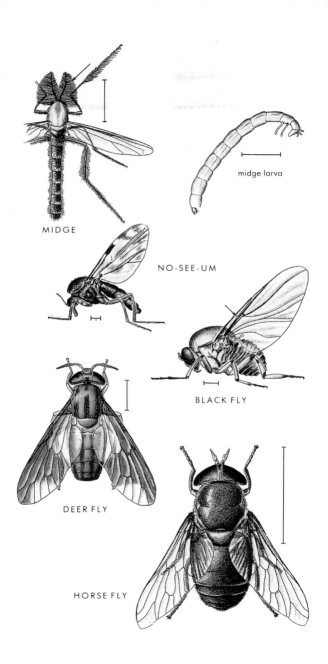

MIDGE

midge larva

NO-SEE-UM

BLACK FLY

DEER FLY

HORSE FLY

ROBBER FLIES range in size from ³/₁₆ to more than 1 inch long. Most have a *long, tapering abdomen* connected to a roughly *spherical thorax*. Most of these flies are not very colorful. Many are quite *bristly*, and a few species look and sound just like bumblebees. Robber flies catch prey in the air. They perch on leaves or on the ground until a potential meal comes within range. Then they dart out and grasp their prey in their long, powerful legs, immobilize it with their stout beak, and suck out the victim's juices. They occur in a wide range of habitats, attacking many different kinds of insects. They seem to prefer species as large or larger than themselves. Robber fly larvae are predators in soil and decaying wood. The adults do not attack people, but if handled carelessly they can give an unforgettable bite.

BEE FLIES are unlikely to be mistaken for any other kind of insect, though their *stout, hairy bodies* may seem more bee-like than fly-like. Many bee flies have very *long, beak-like mouth parts* and look like hummingbirds as they hover in midair and probe into flowers. Some species are quite elegant, with *patterned wings* and *black and silver body hairs*. Bee fly larvae are parasites, feeding on the larvae or eggs of wasps, beetles, grasshoppers, and other insects.

LONG-LEGGED FLIES. These small flies do have *long legs*, but the most striking thing about the majority of long-legged flies is their brilliantly shiny *metallic coloration*. The larvae live in wet soil, rotten wood, under bark, and in plant stems. In some species they catch prey. Adults are very common. You may find them perched on vegetation near wetlands or in meadows. They capture and eat small, soft-bodied insects.

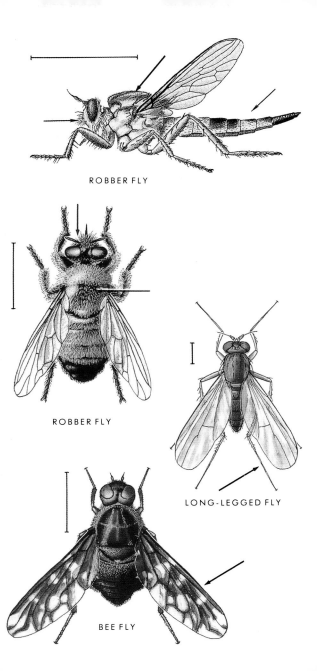

ROBBER FLY

ROBBER FLY

LONG-LEGGED FLY

BEE FLY

FLOWER FLIES OR SYRPHIDS. Anyone who does not believe that flies can be beautiful should become acquainted with this large family. Many of its members are very common on flowers from early spring until late in the fall. A great many syrphids are patterned in *black* and *yellow* and closely *resemble various wasps.* Some are so like their models that they are easy to mistake. Many syrphid larvae thrive in polluted water, where few other living things can survive. Others live in ant nests, eating the hosts' excrement, or in dung, carrion, or rotting plants. A few feed on live plants or prey on aphids (p. 50). Adult syrphids are probably important as pollinators. They do not feed on blood.

FRUIT FLIES AND PICTURE-WINGED FLIES are all *small* to *medium-sized*, often with *colorful bodies* and highly *patterned wings.* Members of both families also tend to perch in a sunny spot and move their wings as if in display. The larval habits of picture-winged flies are not well known, but some feed on plants. The adults are often abundant, especially in moist habitats. Some fruit fly larvae are agricultural pests. The Apple Maggot and the Mediterranean Fruit Fly (Medfly) are well known to fruit growers. Other fruit fly larvae are gall makers and leaf miners. For other "fruit flies," see pomace flies (next group).

POMACE OR FRUIT FLIES are familiar to anyone who has left old fruit or vegetables out too long. They are usually *yellowish* and only ⅛ *inch long.* The larvae feed on yeasts and molds that grow on decaying plants. Because pomace flies can be reared in large numbers in the laboratory, they are useful in genetic research. In the wild, they are important as scavengers and aid in the natural fermentation of grapes.

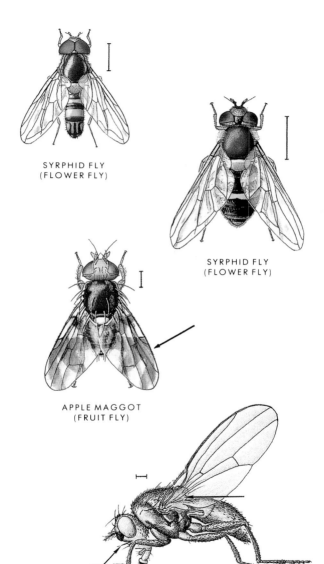

SYRPHID FLY
(FLOWER FLY)

SYRPHID FLY
(FLOWER FLY)

APPLE MAGGOT
(FRUIT FLY)

POMACE FLY

BOT AND WARBLE FLIES parasitize various animals and are well known to people who have horses, cattle, or other livestock. These flies are *medium-sized* to *large*, and the hairier species look like bees. The Ox Warble Fly attaches its eggs to hairs on a cow's legs. The larvae burrow into the animal's flesh and travel upwards for months until they rest under the skin of the cow's back. The inch-long larvae become enclosed in cysts called "warbles." When mature they break through the host's skin and pupate in the ground. These pests cause weight loss and milk reduction in cattle. Certain bot flies lay their eggs in the nostrils of sheep and other animals.

HOUSE FLIES, BLOW FLIES, AND OTHERS.
The insects that most people consider to be "ordinary" flies belong to a number of different families. The best-known of these is the House Fly, disliked for its habits of breeding in filth and its role in spreading diseases. Adult House Flies feed by lapping up liquids. Stable Flies look just like House Flies, but feed by sucking blood. Their human victims are usually surprised to find that "house flies" can bite.

Bright *metallic blue* or *green* blow flies ("bluebottles" and "greenbottles") lay their eggs mainly on animal carcasses and other dead tissue. A few species feed on live animals and are pests in stockyards. Blow flies are important in disposing of organic wastes.

Tachinid flies make up one of the largest families of flies. Most species are *bristly* and larger than House Flies. Tachinids parasitize other insects, including many pests. The eggs hatch within the body of the female. The larvae are placed on the host insect or on the host's food plant, where they wait to be eaten by the host. Adult tachinids commonly visit flowers. They do not bite.

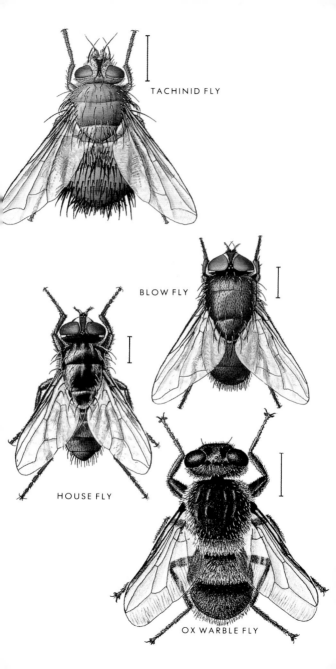

TACHINID FLY

BLOW FLY

HOUSE FLY

OX WARBLE FLY

FLEAS are *very small* (generally less than 3/16 inch long), *wingless* insects with a *hard, dark-colored body* that has *flattened sides.* This combination of characteristics, together with their habit of *jumping* many times their length, is unique to fleas.

As anyone with a fur-bearing pet knows, fleas are blood-sucking parasites. They sometimes live in carpets and furniture, and take an occasional meal from a human host. Some species of fleas feed on birds, but most are found mammals. Unlike lice, fleas are highly mobile and often not particular about what species they visit.

Eggs are laid in the dirt or fall off the host and hatch on the ground. The larvae are *slender, whitish,* and *legless,* with a *well-developed head* and *2 hooks* at the tip of the body. Flea larvae develop on the ground, eating organic debris, and pupate in a silken cocoon.

A number of diseases are transmitted by fleas, including epidemic typhus and bubonic plague. Fleas also carry tapeworms from dogs and rodents and occasionally transmit them to humans.

DOG FLEA

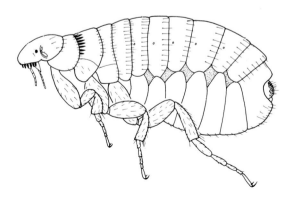

WASPS, ANTS, AND BEES. Except for wingless forms (ants and the females of certain wasps), the members of this order are best distinguished from flies by their *2 pairs of wings.* The wings are *transparent, smoky brown,* or *black,* and almost always have a *dark mark on the front edge* of the forewing. Another feature is the relatively *long antennae.* Except for the sawflies and horntails (pp. 109 and 110), most insects in this order are also "*wasp-waisted*"—the abdomen is very narrow where it joins the thorax. Compare them with certain flies, many of which mimic wasps or bees.

This is usually regarded as the most highly evolved order of insects. It is probably best known for the highly developed honey bee and ant societies, but the order also contains many solitary wasps and bees. The majority of wasps are parasites. Their young hatch and develop inside the bodies of other insects or spiders. The larvae of social species such as Honey Bees remain in the nest where the eggs were laid, and are fed by adult members of the colony. Wasps,

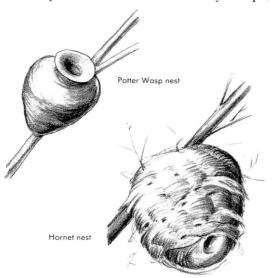

Potter Wasp nest

Hornet nest

ants, and bees occur almost everywhere as adults and feed on a great variety of plants and animals. You are most likely to see them on flowers or around their nests.

A few wasps are timber or orchard pests, carpenter ants damage wooden houses, and the ovipositor of the females of many species has been modified into a sting. However, on the whole this group of insects is highly beneficial to humanity. The parasitic wasps are our chief allies in the control of many pest insects. Bees and wasps pollinate many food crop and horticultural plants.

This order is third in size behind the beetles and the butterflies and moths. It contains 105,000 species worldwide, and 16,300 in North America.

cocoons of Braconid Wasp
on Tomato Hornworm
(sphinx moth larva)

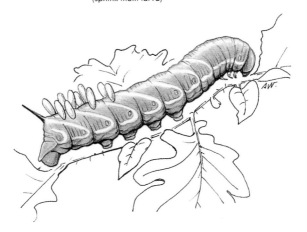

SAWFLIES are wasp-like insects that *lack a "waist"* where the thorax joins the abdomen. The name refers to the *saw-shaped ovipositor* in some species. Some species, such as the Elm Sawfly, resemble bumblebees in shape, though they are not hairy. Sawflies are often *black, brown,* or *red,* and many are *brightly marked in red or yellow.* The larvae are also colorful and resemble caterpillars more than they do the other larvae of their order. Most eat the leaves of trees and shrubs, and a few species bore in fruit, stems, wood, or leaves. The larvae pupate within a cocoon or in a sheltered spot. You will usually find adult sawflies at flowers or near their larval food plants. A few species of sawflies are forest pests, damaging hardwoods and conifers.

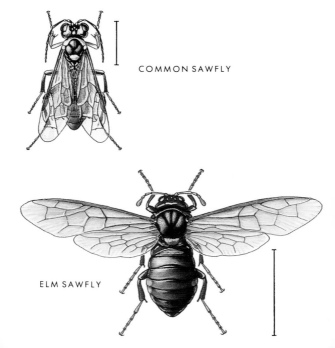

COMMON SAWFLY

ELM SAWFLY

HORNTAILS are closely related to the sawflies. They, too, are *not "wasp-waisted."* You can recognize them by their *long, cylindrical bodies* and *long wings.* Females insert their eggs in tree bark or wood. The larvae are wood borers, but they are not common enough to be serious pests. Despite the imposing ovipositor, horntails do not sting.

ICHNEUMONS are *slender, elegant,* often *colorful* wasps. They make up one of the largest of insect families, with 3000 North American species. The females of most species have *long ovipositors.*

Different groups of ichneumons tend to specialize in parasitizing particular families of insects or spiders, and few families escape this attack. Females usually insert their eggs into the eggs, larvae, or pupae of other insects. The larvae feed and pupate within the host. To reach the galleries where larvae of wood-boring beetles or other hosts are found, the females must sometimes penetrate up to ½ inch of wood with their needle-thin ovipositors. Ichneumons are extremely valuable in the control of pest species.

Adult ichneumons often visit flowers. Larger species with shorter, stouter ovipositors can give a mild sting.

BRACONIDS are *small* to *tiny* wasps, closely related to the ichneumons, though they tend to be stouter and are seldom brightly colored. They are abundant, and many species help control pest insects. Braconid larvae often pupate in little silken cocoons that usually occur in clusters on or away from the host. Most vegetable gardeners will have seen tomato hornworms covered with these cocoons (see p. 108).

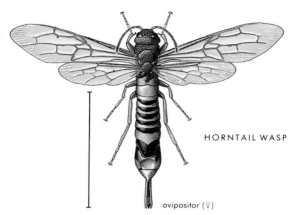

HORNTAIL WASP

ovipositor (♀)

ICHNEUMON WASP

ovipositor (♀)

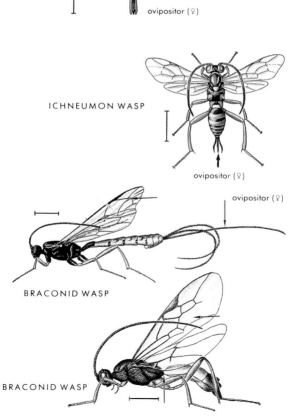

ovipositor (♀)

BRACONID WASP

BRACONID WASP

CHALCIDS are abundant, highly beneficial, and often beautiful insects. You may not be aware of them, however, because most of them are *tiny.* Chalcids are perhaps the supreme parasites. Their small size enables them to lay eggs in tiny insect eggs, in pupae, or in adults of very small insects such as aphids. Many species produce up to 1000 young from a single egg. Many species are also parasites of other parasites. Chalcids may enter their hosts by means other than inserting eggs. For example, eggs may be deposited on the food plant of a moth larva or caterpillar, where they will be swallowed as the caterpillar feeds. Chalcids mainly parasitize butterflies and moths, flies, beetles, and hoppers. Since these orders contain most of our worst crop pests, these tiny wasps are very helpful to humanity.

GALL WASPS. A gall is an enlarged growth of plant tissue. It occurs in response to a chemical secreted by an insect. You may have seen some common galls—lumps on the stems of goldenrod plants or on oak leaves. Most of the approximately 800 North American species of this family make galls or live in galls made by other organisms. Each species creates a gall on a particular part of a particular type of plant, and the form of the gall is usually more distinctive than the insect itself. Most galls are made by wasps and flies, but some are produced by beetles, moths, aphids, mites, and even fungi.

In most cases it is the chemical secreted by the larva as it grows that stimulates the plant to produce the extra tissue that forms the gall. The gall provides the larva with food, shelter, and moisture. Few types of galls injure the plants on which they grow. Many gall wasps are specific to oak trees, and some oak galls are a source of dyes and tannic acid.

CHALCID WASP

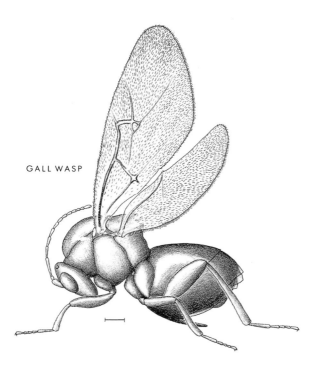

GALL WASP

Oak apple gall
made by Gall Wasp

CUCKOO WASPS are *small,* very handsome insects, colored bright *metallic blue, green, or purple.* You can usually tell them apart from similar wasps and bees by the *punctures* and other *coarse sculpturing* of their body surface. Cuckoo wasps are named for their habit of laying their eggs in the nests of bees or other wasps, much as the European Cuckoo lays its eggs in the nests of other birds. The cuckoo wasp larva waits until the host larva is full grown, and then feeds on it externally. Host species apparently recognize cuckoo wasps as enemies and attack them. The parasites respond to attack by folding up into a ball. Adult cuckoo wasps often visit flowers.

VELVET ANTS are *wasps* rather than true ants, though the wingless females look similar to ants. They are always covered in a *short, thick coat of hairs,* and they are usually *brightly colored* in *red, orange,* or *yellow.* Velvet ants are parasites, mainly on ground-nesting bees and wasps, though beetles and flies are also known to be hosts. Females of this family are notorious for their very painful stings.

SPIDER WASPS. The best known members of this family are the "tarantula hawks" of the Southwest, which reach more than 1½ inches in length and are often strikingly colored in *blue-black* and *rusty red.* There are many smaller species throughout the rest of the continent, however. You can often see them on flowers or on the ground, searching for prey. This is mainly spiders, which the wasps paralyze with their sting. The wasps put the prey in burrows in the ground and lay an egg on each spider. The larvae feed on the spider after they emerge. Spider wasps can inflict a powerful sting, but are not aggressive.

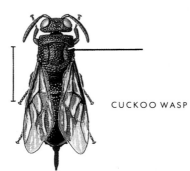

CUCKOO WASP

VELVET ANT

♀

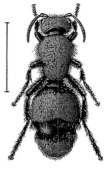

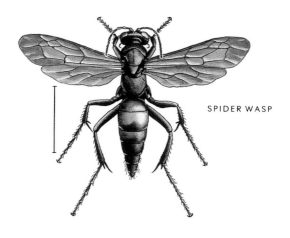

SPIDER WASP

VESPID WASPS. This large family contains many common species. The better-known subgroups are described below.

POTTER WASPS are solitary wasps, mostly ½–¾ *inch long* and *black* with *white or yellow* markings. Some species make beautiful little *jug-shaped nests* of mud, which they attach to twigs. Others nest in ground burrows or other cavities. Most potter wasps stock their nests with caterpillars that they have paralyzed to feed their larvae. They lay their eggs near the food insects, which they suspend on threads from the cell walls.

HORNETS AND YELLOWJACKETS need little introduction to most people. They are social wasps that have evolved powerful stings and aggressive behavior for defending their colonies. Since they are very common and frequently nest in or near buildings, these traits often bring them into confrontations with their human neighbors. All of these wasps build *complex nests of "paper"* that they make by chewing bits of wood or leaves. The most familiar of these nests are the round ones made by the Bald-faced Hornet. These are often cemented under the eaves of houses or barns, or hung from branches of trees or shrubs. Most yellowjackets nest in the ground. Like other social insects, these wasps have a "caste" system made up of queens, males, and sterile female workers. Where winter is harsh, all die off except for the queens, which hibernate in tree cavities, walls, or other shelter. They begin new colonies by themselves the following spring. The larvae are reared in the cells of the nest and are fed chewed-up insects and other "meat" by the workers. These wasps do not hesitate to attack if they sense a threat to their nest. They can inflict a very painful sting, causing an allergic reaction in some victims.

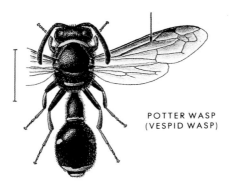

POTTER WASP
(VESPID WASP)

HORNET
(VESPID WASP)

YELLOWJACKET
(VESPID WASP)

PAPER WASPS. These insects have the graceful *wasp-waisted* form and *long dangling legs* that most people think of when the word "wasp" is mentioned. They are usually an inch or more long and *brown or reddish* overall, sometimes with *yellow markings.* Their nests are typically a *single tier* of "paper" cells attached to the eaves of a building or similar surface by a short stem. The habits of paper wasps are generally similar to those of the hornets and yellowjackets. Though they have a strong sting, they are not aggressive.

SPHECID WASPS. This is another large family containing many colorfully patterned, familiar wasps. All are solitary and stock a cavity nest with a particular type of prey to feed their larvae. They paralyze the prey by stinging it, and lay an egg on it. The thread-waisted wasps are named for their distinctively shaped abdomen. One of the most common of these is the large, shiny blue-black Mud Dauber that often sticks its masonry nest cells on buildings. This species stocks its nest with paralyzed spiders. Most thread-waisted wasps excavate burrows in the ground and provide their larvae with caterpillars or grasshoppers. Other sphecids nest in hollowed-out twigs, abandoned galleries created by wood-boring beetles, and other cavities in wood. Few groups of insects are not preyed upon by these interesting and beneficial wasps. The adults commonly visit flowers.

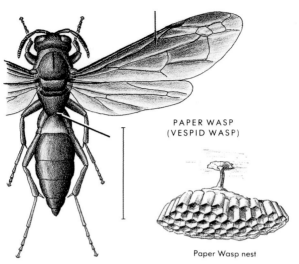

PAPER WASP
(VESPID WASP)

Paper Wasp nest

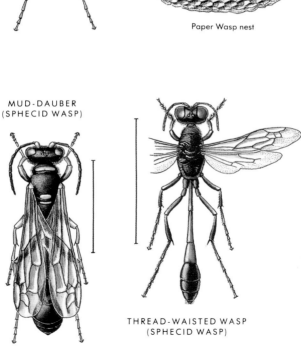

MUD-DAUBER
(SPHECID WASP)

THREAD-WAISTED WASP
(SPHECID WASP)

ANTS may be the most abundant of all land animals. North American ant species come in a wide range of sizes and colors *(black, brown, red, yellowish, and combinations* of these.) It is the behavior of ants, however, rather than their appearance, that has long fascinated people. All ants are social insects, and colonies of various species may consist of from dozens to thousands of ants. Most ant colonies consist of three castes: one or more large queens, which lay all the eggs; a few small males, which are produced periodically and mate with the queen(s); and many sterile female workers, which form the majority of the colony. New queens and males have wings, and mate in periodic flights. The "flying ants" that you might see in spring are mostly these winged males. They die soon after the queen has mated. After the mating flight, a new queen sheds her wings and either starts a new colony or enters an established colony. Most ants nest in the ground, though there are many tree-nesting species. Nests vary greatly in size and form.

Most ants eat animals, including other insects, but many eat plants or scavenge on whatever is available. A few species are pests. Carpenter ants, the largest North American ants, dig galleries in wood and sometimes damage foundations and other wooden structures. They do not feed on the wood, as do termites. Fire ants of the Southeast kill and eat nesting birds, including young poultry, and cause much distress to other livestock. Many ants also destroy other pest insects, and are a great food source for birds and other animals.

FIRE ANT

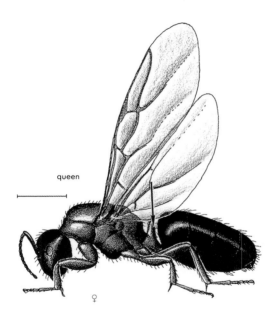

queen

♀

CARPENTER ANT

♂

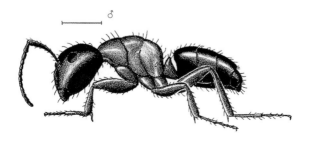

BEES can generally be distinguished from other members of the order by their overall *hairiness,* though there are some hairy wasps and relatively hairless bees. Another characteristic of most bees is *enlarged, flattened segments of the hind legs.* One of these pairs of segments is typically *fringed* with *long, stiff hairs* and used for carrying pollen.

In their nesting habits bees are very similar to wasps. One important difference, however, is that bee larvae are fed honey and pollen instead of animal tissue. Pollen is collected on the body hairs of bees as they probe in flowers for nectar. They comb off the pollen with the fringed hind leg segments and store it either in these "pollen baskets" or on the underside of the abdomen. Honey is nectar that has been modified by enzymes in the digestive system of the bees and then ripened in the hive.

Bees are by far the most important of insect pollinators. This service is vital to most orchard fruits and berries, many vegetables and field crops, and flowers. The best-known bees are the bumble bees and the Honey Bee, both of which nest in colonies. However, most of the 3300 North American bee species are solitary nesters. A few major groups of bees are described below.

SWEAT BEE

SWEAT BEES make up a large family of *small to medium-sized* bees. Some are *dark red* or brilliant *metallic green* or *blue*, but many are *brown or blackish*. They nest in the ground, typically laying eggs in a series of branching tunnels. They are not social bees, but often dig their burrows close together in open areas, forming loose colonies. A few species are attracted by human perspiration; hence the name sweat bees. You may frequently find them at flowers.

LEAFCUTTING BEE

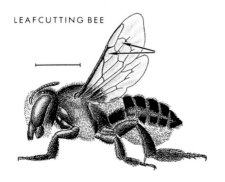

CARPENTER BEES closely resemble bumble bees except for their abdomen, which is completely *black*, relatively *hairless*, and *shiny*. The larger species chew nest burrows out of solid wood, sometimes damaging houses and other structures. You can often see them hovering near their nest holes, engaging in territorial combat with other members of their species. Smaller carpenter bees make a series of nest cells by removing the pith from woody shrubs and walling off sections of the resulting tunnel.

BUMBLE BEES. The *fat, furry, black and yellow* form of these bees is familiar to everyone. Except for a few species that lay their eggs in the nests of other bumble bees, these are social bees. Like other societies in this order, bumble bee colonies contain queens, drones (males), and sterile female workers. All species nest in holes in the ground, often in abandoned rodents' nests. They construct a waxen comb in which to rear young. Only queens survive the winter, and these produce the first generation of workers on their own early in the spring. Certain species of red clover can only be pollinated by the exceptionally long tongues of bumble bees. These large bees can deliver a painful sting, but they are not aggressive unless their nests are approached too closely.

LARGE CARPENTER BEE

SMALL CARPENTER BEE

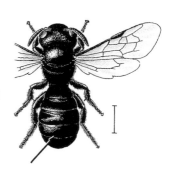

BUMBLE BEE

HONEY BEES. Our best-known bee is a single social species first introduced from Europe during the colonial period. Our most important pollinators, most Honey Bees still live in manmade hives, but many wild colonies also thrive, usually in hollow trees. Unlike most social bees and wasps, all of the castes in Honey Bee colonies survive through the winter. In fact, new hives cannot be started by the queen alone. A hive normally contains only a single queen. A new queen is produced by feeding a larva a special type of food. She may be killed by the reigning queen or one of the two may fly off with part of the colony and start a new hive. The only other occasion on which the queen leaves the hive is to engage in a mating flight with the drones. These males are produced for this purpose alone, and only one succeeds in mating. Drones remaining in the colony after the queen has been fertilized are killed by the workers.

Because of their economic importance, Honey Bees have been extensively studied. Among other interesting discoveries, a form of bee "language" has been observed. An individual that finds a good source of nectar can give directions to it by doing a complex dance, and indicate the species of flower by the smell of a sample of nectar.

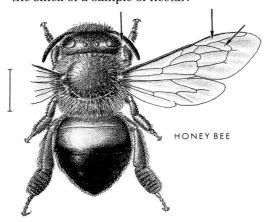

HONEY BEE

INDEX

Color illustrations of the insects generally appear on the page facing the text.